Ba.
wo1
His _____ _____ Scripture always
bring, _____ because it contains everything we
need for life and godliness (2 Peter 1:3). For this
reason, you should read, "Balance" by my friend
Sarena Braudrick. And as you do, you'll begin to
feel like it is just you and a good friend, sitting
across a table from one another, talking about
what it means to follow Christ in a messed up
world sorely in need of recalibration. Sarena
writes with passion and insight, both heat and
light. Listen to her talk about her journey toward
balance and I promise you that you will find help
for your own.

Dr. Brett Selby
Pastoral Leadership Specialist
Baptist General Convention of Oklahoma

As a recovering addict, I understand the
ramifications of a life out of balance. In this Bible
study, Sarena will gracefully guide you through
a series of steps that perfectly prepare you to
keep your life equally distributed. Setting you
up to live the free and abundant life God always
intended you to live. As Sarena unpacks the
wisdom found in 1 Peter 1:5-7, she will instill in
you a hope that a life of freedom and purpose is
within your grasp. No longer do we need to be
tossed around from the waves of this world. Now
we have a guide that will help keep us grounded

and balanced. This is a must read for anyone trying to properly balance their life in a world that glorifies busyness and praises excess.

Lance Lang
Founder of Hope Is Alive Ministries

Balance is a remarkably applicable study that relates so deeply to the life of the everyday woman. It helps us to wrestle with the hard questions and solve the unrelenting problems we face on a daily basis, while teaching us how to find ourselves and how to believe in ourselves once again. This book had such an impact on me, that when I went through the study and inched closer to the end, I knew I couldn't stop there. I immediately fostered another group of women and shared with them this amazing and pertinent material. This is a must read and a must share!

Keli Barbee
Wife, mother, daughter, friend, graphic designer, and online education specialist

BALANCE

Pursuing God in an Ungodly World

BALANCE

SARENA BRAUDRICK

TATE PUBLISHING
AND ENTERPRISES, LLC

Published by Tate Publishing & Enterprises, LLC
127 E. Trade Center Terrace | Mustang, Oklahoma 73064 USA
1.888.361.9473 | www.tatepublishing.com

Tate Publishing is committed to excellence in the publishing industry. The company reflects the philosophy established by the founders, based on Psalm 68:11,
"The Lord gave the word and great was the company of those who published it."

Book design copyright © 2014 by Tate Publishing, LLC. All rights reserved.
Cover design by Rodrigo Adolfo
Interior design by Mary Jean Archival

Published in the United States of America
ISBN: 978-1-63268-220-8
Religion / Christian Life / Women's Issues
14.09.29

To my husband, Bob, the toughest and most formidable cheerleader the world has ever known.

ACKNOWLEDGMENTS

Shannon Yousey, Julie Perdue, Linda Koop, and Wendell Lang—Thank you for your time, your thoughts, and your prayers.

Deborah Newport and the Tuesday Night Ladies Bible Study Group—Thank you for your obedience to God's calling. You have been a constant source of love and encouragement.

To my family—You give me such great joy and inspiration. I love you!

Thank you Lord. You lead me and direct my steps. You put a song in my heart and a message on my lips. You are my great provider. I am overwhelmed by your perfect love.

FOREWORD

I love this book and you will also. Balance is a
characteristic that we all need to consider. It is essential
to quality leadership and effective discipleship. What
better quest could we have than to have healthy balance
in our Christian life. There are three things that today's
younger generation are attracted to: solid Bible study, a
transparent spirit, and vulnerability in telling one's story.
Sarena has captured all of these elements in her book.
Her explanation of scripture will cause you to want to
study the scripture on your own. She has candidly and
openly given you an insider's view into her own life.
Furthermore, she has a way of being self-deprecating
that puts the reader at ease, and this makes you want to
engage even further.

A good writer has a way of making the deep content
seem approachable and understandable. I was so moved
by this book that I have read it twice, and plan on reading
it again. You will be challenged and charged up to have

a well-rounded life. You will be inspired to trim off the rough edges of your life. Balance will not only be a benign phrase reserved for the few, but you will find a balanced life attainable and desirable. It has been my privilege to pastor Sarena and her precious family for several years. I can testify that she lives out what she has written. She typifies the qualities embodied in this book. After you read it, hopefully, you will find balance the new normal in your own life.

Dr. Wendell Lang, senior pastor of Surrey Hills Baptist Church

CONTENTS

INTRODUCTION

So make every effort to apply the benefits of these promises to your life. Then your faith will produce a life of moral excellence. A life of moral excellence leads to knowing God better. Knowing God leads to self-control. Self-control leads to patient endurance, and patient endurance leads to godliness. Godliness leads to love for other Christians, and finally you will grow to have a genuine love for everyone.

2 Peter 1:5–7 (NLT)

Someone once asked me if I had to think of my absolute favorite passage of scripture, what would it be? That's a loaded question. There are so many scriptures that are unbelievably powerful in so many differing ways. But in the end, I'd have to say 2 Peter 1:5–7, and this is why: I don't think there is any other scripture that in a matter of just three verses gives you the secret to godly maturity and understanding in such an applicable way. It lays out genuine peace and joy in just eight steps. I am in no way trying to minimize these steps as easy. If you're familiar with a twelve-step program for recovery from addiction, you *know* that those steps aren't easy, but their completion is necessary for healing and wholeness. And so it goes, if you really want to know God, if you really want to know freedom from the pain and bondage of sin, if you really want to know true understanding and forgiveness, and if you really want to truly love the way God loves, these steps are necessary.

Meditating on these three passages is one of the most precise tools for measuring where you are relationally with God. Look closely at these three verses. They are actually eight individual steps.

1. So make every effort to apply the benefits of these promises to your life.
2. Then your faith will produce a life of moral excellence.
3. A life of moral excellence leads to knowing God better.
4. Knowing God leads to self-control.
5. Self-control leads to patient endurance.
6. Patient endurance leads to godliness.
7. Godliness leads to love for other Christians.
8. Finally, you will grow to have a genuine love for everyone.

When I analyze these eight steps, I can determine where I've detoured and where I've been faithful. For example, if I get to step five and really evaluate myself and say, "Wow! I genuinely have trouble exercising self-control in my own life," then I not only know where I detoured, but I also *now* know to ask, "Why?" Why did I walk away here? Was it too scary? Was I too into myself? What is it about me that made me want to stop here, instead of going all the way with God? In contrast, you can measure how far your faith has taken you, and you can see all the greatness that God has done in you. Either way, God wants a life full of blessings and freedom for you. It's a life that, on your own, you cannot experience or even dream up, but if we make the choice to know God fully, and we don't jump ship, He really will show us a life so good and so meaningful, we couldn't have even imagined it ourselves.

One Sunday, I had the privilege of teaching these three verses to a group of high school students. That experience inspired me to begin writing some of what was said, and what was left unsaid in that youth room on Sunday morning.

It's all about…balance.

WEEK ONE

BALANCE

My husband tells the story to all of our children of what he was taught at Welcome Week by the dean of students his first few days at college. The dean shared that college could be one of the most inspiring times in their lives if they strived to live a balanced life. He said if they loved God, worked hard, stayed fit, and got involved, God would use this time to ignite their passion so they might live a truly meaningful life. Spiritual, mental, physical, and social—these are the four parts of us. Think of these four parts in a circle all connected to one another, with God being the center.

These elements are in all people, and it is His hope that we would live out our God-given potential *with Him* and *through Him*. When we don't, our lives are out of balance. We are seemingly lost, frustrated, and confused as to our purpose and our direction.

No one is *trying* to live an unbalanced life. There are circumstances and/or experiences that can unknowingly steer us into a life teetering on the high wire, and inevitably plummeting into the net below. The reasons we live a life out of balance are formed in our minds and hearts, just as surely as our root belief systems. Trauma, ignorance, and complacency are used by our enemy to bind us to a life unfulfilled and unrealized.

For example:

> Trauma—Did the death of a loved one send you spiraling into depression, addiction, and/or hopelessness?
> Complacency—Did your peers or family members marginalize you, causing you to feel like you had only an average ability to learn…so you just stopped trying?
> Ignorance—Do you not even know to contemplate your spiritual life, because no one has ever taken you

under their wing, and shown you that you are more than just a wandering being without purpose?

A variety of negative life experiences can pilot us into an unbalanced life, but it is only a relationship with God that can bring us back into balance with Him and with ourselves.

SPIRITUAL

Let's tackle the spiritual. Everything we are is spiritual. In fact, everything we are and everything we do is supposed to be blanketed by God. What I mean is when we are connected with Him and walking day by day in His presence, then paying your electric bill is spiritual, driving your kids to school is spiritual, walking on your treadmill is spiritual, lunch with your girlfriend is spiritual. Why? Let me answer with a story. I know a professor who spends around three hours a week writing recommendation letters for his students. He said that sometimes he is tempted to huff and puff and bemoan having to write these letters, but then he quickly remembers that *because* he writes these letters that one student might be accepted into law school, love God, raise children, give generously, and make a difference. Another might be given the opportunity to go into the mission field and change the world for Christ. Another might be able to get the job of her dreams and then have the means to care for her ailing parents. His recommendation letters *mean* something. They might seem very small in the grand scheme of things, but they play a huge part in expanding the kingdom of God.

God wants us to live our lives with Him. So when we are washing our seventeenth load of laundry, we're doing it with Him and for Him, and it matters. It's spiritual. He wants to be where we are, and He wants you to be where He is. He wants to be so intertwined with us that He is our first thought for every joyful moment, whether it's just recognizing the beauty of a cloudless day, or celebrating a huge promotion at work. He wants to be our first thought during the painful moments too. No matter how big or small—the pain a mother feels when her child tells her she was picked on at school today, or the devastating loss of a loved one, or the loneliness of a broken marriage— God wants to be in the middle of it all because He loves us so entirely. Ephesians 3:17–19 says,

> And I pray that Christ will be more and more at home in your hearts as you trust in Him. May your roots go down deep into the soil of God's marvelous love. And may you have the power to understand, as all God's people should, how wide, how long, how high, and how deep His love really is. May you experience the love of Christ, though it is so great you will never fully understand it. Then you will be filled with the fullness of life and power that comes from God.

Love so marvelous, so deep, that we will never fully get it, but if we let God be more at home in us, we will be filled with fullness of life and God's power…sign me up! When we connect with Him then our spiritual being is balanced. When we are disconnected, then everything is disconnected, and we are not functioning at full capacity. We're out of balance.

- Are you "doing" life with God?

  _____

- Is God at home in your heart?

  _____

- If not, then why? (be honest and authentic)

  _____
  _____

- What practical things could you do to make yourself more available to His desires for your life?

  _____
  _____

- Name two tasks that you do at least twice a week. Evaluate your attitude toward completing these tasks. Commit to regarding them as spiritual. How will doing that change you and the people around you?

  _____
  _____

PHYSICAL

Now even if you are doing your life with God, you can still be "out of balance." Of that I am living proof. Obviously, taking care of the vessel that has been loaned to you while you live on this earth is important. Eating right, exercise…

that's a given. That's spiritual, because our bodies are spiritual. If God lives in our bodies and God provided our bodies to us, then how could they not be? And still obesity is the leading cause of illness in America, and I have struggled with this for decades. I have a friend who calls habitual overeating the Christian's "turn a blind eye" sin. We justify it, accept it, but in doing so we destroy our bodies. I love God, walk with Him, I'm close to Him, and dedicating my body to Him has been a lifelong struggle. Whether I like it or not, my unwillingness to give God ultimate domain makes me unbalanced. On a more drastic level, dealing with the devastating consequences of abusing our bodies chemically or sexually by living outside God's parameters, leaves us not only unbalanced, but broken. Understanding that our spirit, our bodies, and our minds are all interconnected helps us to understand that what we do to our bodies we do to our Spirit, God's spirit.

Do you view your body as spiritual?

_____

In what kinds of ways do you care for your body?

_____

_____

Can you describe a time when you didn't treat your body like the temple of God. How has God changed and healed you?

_____

_____

In what ways could you be better honoring your body?

_____

_____

MENTAL

You might ask: why does God care if I challenge myself mentally? Surely this is something we just tell our kids so they will make straight As in school, do well on the ACTs, and get a scholarship to college. While, let me tell you, as the mother of a college student, that's really nice, it is not God's number one purpose for mental growth. God wants us to be intelligent. He wants us to have great understanding, to be wise, to be successful, to achieve. When we are growing our minds in God, whether through His Word or through chemistry or accounting or sonnets by William Shakespeare, we are stimulating this wondrous organ God created called the brain. Our brain is physical and spiritual and can be used to do great things with God and for God. We are built to thirst for knowledge. We should live to learn of God's creations and plans.

This does not take three college degrees to achieve. I love the line from the movie *Good Will Hunting* when our seemingly simpleminded hero is confronted with a Harvard-educated snob. The lead character, Will, schools this guy—I mean humiliates him in a debate and then says, "You know, you dropped a 150 grand on an education you could have gotten for $1.50 in late charges at the public library." Don't be intimidated into thinking if you didn't score a 12,000 on your SATs, or you didn't graduate from some fancy college that God just doesn't need you to grow mentally. Growing mentally in God will bring you closer to Him, and also assist you in changing the world for Him.

> We ask God to give you a complete understanding of what he wants to do in your lives, and we ask him to make you wise with spiritual wisdom. Then the way you live will always please and honor the Lord, and you will continually do good, kind things for others. All the while you will *learn* to know God better.
>
> Colossians 1:9–10 (ɴʟᴛ)

Learning, knowing, understanding...God wants you to use your head. In contrast, pseudo-intellectualism is seriously overrated (we'll talk more about that later), but understanding and wisdom are priceless. If we are not striving to learn, we are out of balance. Side note: If you are filling your mind with garbage, you are counteracting God's purposes. So if you are watching any show with a Kardashian in it...*stop!*

Do you dedicate time to developing your mind?

In what ways?

Do you see room for improvement and if so, what kinds of things inspire you to do some deeper thinking? (discussion, reading, lectures, etc.)

In what ways might you be counteracting growth with useless knowledge?

_____

_____

SOCIAL

We, by nature, are social creatures. Some of us are more naturally inclined to social situations than others. We all know that lady who always knows the right thing to say, at exactly the right time, to make everyone in the room feel accepted and comfortable. She is described as a people person. Others of us are a little more socially awkward. Those "people person" abilities baffle us. So we have to *learn* to be social. Why? Because we were created to love one another and to connect with one another. How are we going to do that if we don't leave the house or talk to anyone? Scripture tells us we need to teach others, encourage others, listen to others, be interested in others, and love others (Phi. 2:1–4).

My daughter, Katie, is in her freshman year at college, and while she is not always motivated to get out there and engage with people, she makes it a point to discipline herself to be around people regularly. She noticed several girls in her dorm hall who never came out of their rooms. Even when invited to grab a pizza, they would politely decline. They went home every weekend, didn't go to the Bible studies, didn't go to the football games, and didn't come back for the second semester. Why? They didn't engage. They didn't make relationships. There is a statistic that claims 80 percent of people who don't find a small group in their church will be gone within two years. We need people, and people need us.

Lydia was a successful merchant in Thyatira. She worshipped God and was baptized by Paul in Acts 16:14–16. She recognized the need for healthy relationships in her life, and so she urged Paul and his missionaries to stay in her home until they agreed. The NIV translation says, "that she *prevailed* upon them." I love the word *prevailed*. It means that she pursued those relationships. We need to be pursuing lasting relationships. God is sending people into our lives, but are we accepting them or rejecting them? 1 John 1:7 says, "But if we are living in the light of God's presence, just as Christ is, then we have fellowship with each other." I thank God that He has placed mature people in my life who have forgiven my flaws and immaturity. I tell people all the time that I am blessed with the most wonderful, godly, patient friends for which any woman could ever ask. Making these deep and lasting friendships has taken many years, but it has been worth every awkward, uncomfortable, nervous moment. If we don't engage with others, we are out of balance.

Would you describe yourself as a social person?

_____

If yes, then are your relationships spiritually healthy?

_____

Name three adjectives that describe a spiritually healthy relationship.

_____

_____

If you're not social, then why? Is it fear? Or maybe you've been you've burned, or perhaps it's something else?

_____

_____

Are you prevailing upon people that you know would strengthen you?

_____

What could you do this week to prevail upon another woman you believe could be a godly friend and mentor? Lunch date? Joining a small group? Play date with the kids at McDonald's?

_____

_____

AM I BALANCED?

You might be asking yourself: "Am I a balanced person?" Chances are you're not. Welcome to the club. Neither am I. I'm on the journey, the journey to transparent and meaningful godliness. I may never get there this side of Heaven, but I will keep on keeping on. I want the words of my mouth and the meditations of my heart to be pleasing to Him! When we fall in love with Jesus, this desire arises in our souls to grow and love and change the world for Him. It's only when we let ourselves become our own roadblock that His plans for our lives are squandered. Let's get out of the way, let God be God, and craft us into His own image. Otherwise, the masterful plan that Jesus has for us goes unrealized.

WEEK TWO

"E" FOR EFFORT
STEP 1: "SO MAKE EVERY EFFORT TO APPLY THE BENEFITS OF THESE PROMISES TO YOUR LIFE"

What is God's greatest promise? God made some pretty incredible promises to us. One of the students in our Sunday school class replied, "God will never leave us or forsake us." Another said, halfway kidding, "He'll never flood the earth again." She's right, He won't. But the absolute greatest promise is the gift of His salvation through the belief in His Son, Jesus Christ.

So what does it mean to "make every effort to apply the benefits" of His salvation? There are many different ways to answer that question, but the first answer that came to my mind is actually the example of a student in my class named Erica. Erica came to Falls Creek Christian Camp with our church as a guest when she was thirteen. It was there that she asked God to be her best friend. Erica began to experience something that all new believers experience: an unquenchable thirst and hunger to love and know the God that saved her. She knew she needed Him, but more importantly she "wanted" Him. She wanted to be nourished and transformed. That desire is what I believe "making every effort to apply the benefits of His promises" means. Don't be confused…it's not a set of rules and regulations as some would have you believe. It's passionate, life-changing love.

Sadly, it's on the first step that so many young believers take a detour. I asked these students, "How many kids do you know that walked away right here?" The answer was of course, many. Why? Why walk away before you even get started? The answer was essentially this: it's easy to ask God to come into your life and forgive you, but what happens next is the hard part. What will your classmates think, your parents, your friends, your coworkers about this new desire in your heart, and the decision that you have made to know God? That is often too frightening to face, and so the new believer detours onto the more commonly walked road instead of the road of newness and victory. They believe God saved them, and at the same time, still believe they are enslaved to this world, even though God has set them free.

Priscilla Shirer is a gifted Bible teacher out of Dallas, Texas, and she gives a very daunting illustration of this kind of prison in her Bible study entitled "One in a Million." She and her family had just been to the circus. They saw the trapeze artists, the clowns, the animals; and they had a great time. As they were in their car leaving the parking lot, her young son saw behind the chain link fence an enormous elephant held to the ground by a measly and weak chain. Her son knew the elephant was more powerful than the confines of that chain, and he asked his mother, "Mom, why doesn't that elephant break free? That chain is not strong enough to hold him." She told her son that when the elephant was young, a chain was placed around his ankle from which he could not break free, and as he grew the elephant believed that the chain could not be broken; so even as a gigantic and powerful adult, he still does not believe he can break the chain, even though in reality he could snap it in two with very little effort. The elephant was conditioned. He'd always been enslaved to the deceiving power of that chain. He didn't even *try* to break free. He believed in his perception of himself. In other words, he believed what his surroundings taught him. He was taught by his environment that he was powerless, and therefore that's how he lived—enslaved.

Can you describe an event or circumstance in your own life that has kept you from completely applying the benefits of your salvation?

_____

_____

_____

OR MAYBE IT'S JUST YOUR PRIDE?

Is there a chance you might be smarter than God? People never, and I mean *never* verbalize this. Have you really ever heard someone say, "I'm smarter than God"? Why?

Because they know how ridiculous it sounds. But their belief is revealed in their actions. If this is you…you're busted. Your cover is blown. You reveal yourself by the arrogance in which you live. You might believe that you are more intelligent than the all-knowing God who formed you in your mother's womb, and yet, you may not even realize it yourself. Let me clue you in as a former self-worshiper; if you knowingly choose to believe something contrary to God's Word, you are a self-worshiper. I know that's a difficult thing to admit; it was for me. But if you got real—and I mean *really real*—you would see that the nature of your decisions are based in a belief of yourself, your infallibility, your control, your power. So in essence, you are your own god.

We all know this person. He's that kid who went to college and met all of these incredibly intelligent, cultured people who told him the Bible is "a great read, with some wise and beautiful philosophies, but anyone who believes its inerrant is really very simpleminded." So he becomes estranged to all of the depth and truth he'd been taught, and then replaces it with emptiness disguised as profound intelligence.

Or it's that educated, sophisticated, successful woman who creates her own brand of spirituality. She thinks there *can't* be just one way to God. So she invents ideas that *sound* reasonable to her. These ideas fit her lifestyle. She doesn't need absolutes. She needs a god that will work within her parameters of "comfortable" living.

Are you a little selfish and terrified of commitment? Well then, invent a god that is okay with you living with your significant other out of wedlock. Done. Instead of surrendering your selfish nature, or letting God heal you of your commitment wounds and fears, so you can have a tremendously abundant life blessed by God, you now settle for your version of God—you. In doing so, your life is just second rate. It's never what it could have, should have been.

Listen—I understand what it's like to be in this trap. There were two reasons I fell into this hole: ignorance and fear. Ignorance came from not knowing God or His Word. You don't know what you don't know. The fear came into play because I didn't want to be viewed as "weird" or different, so I stuck to traveling the very wide roads with all the so-called normal folks. I only ended up feeling desperately alone. Proverbs 16:25 says, "There is a way that seems right to man, but in the end it leads to death." Many believers never move past this point, and then they end up drifting and wandering aimlessly into more and more darkness, never understanding that if they had just applied the benefits of their salvation, they could be free. Instead, they settle for a life in captivity chained to the ground, never realizing the power of God only needed to be believed and then used—and the chains would be broken.

Think of yourself in this way—you're a prisoner in an 8x6 jail cell. No light, no room, no freedom. The day finally arrives when you are released. You walk outside, you see the blue sky, smell the pure air, feel the warmth of the sun on your face, and then you turn around and walk right back into that prison. Right back into oppression, captivity, hopelessness. Crazy, right? Hear me—your new life in Christ might be a little intimidating, maybe a lot intimidating, and maybe even a little frightening at times; but outside those walls, your life is limitless, filled with opportunities for joy, success, adventure, love, and newness. Inside the walls, your life is just like your cell—gray, dark, small, wasted.

Can you describe a time in your life—it might even be right now—when you chose to believe in anything contrary to the Word of God. What circumstance in your life led you to that belief?

_____

_____

_____

ME...GOD?

Yes, they knew God, but they wouldn't worship Him as God or even give Him thanks. And they began to think up foolish ideas of what God was like. The result was that their minds became dark and confused. Claiming to be wise, they became utter fools instead. And instead of worshiping the glorious, ever-living God, they worshiped idols made to look like mere people, or birds and animals and snakes. So God let them go ahead and do whatever shameful things their heart desired. As a result they did vile and degrading things with each other's bodies. Instead of believing what they knew was the truth about God, they deliberately chose to believe lies. *So they worshiped the things God made, but not the Creator himself,* who is to be praised forever. Amen.

Romans 1:22–25 (NLT)

There are so many layers to uncover in these scriptures, especially dealing with sexual sin, but I want to zero in on verse 25. These people, normal, everyday people— the people with whom you work, classmates, friends, neighbors, your parents, the lady at the 7-Eleven cash register—believe lies instead of truth. Why? Essentially, because they worship the things that God made, instead of God. Because God made everything, there could be many answers to what people worship, but God's greatest creation was you. God's masterpiece was man. Do you worship yourself? Are your ideas greater than God's? Does what you believe about sex, creation, marriage, politics, business, religion, friendship supersede what God says about all of these things and the universe He created?

People who worship themselves create a god in their own image and then call him "the God." Their god believes what they want and need for him to believe, so their lives will be more comfortable fitting into our society. For example, as a young woman, I was pro-abortion. Why? At the time, I was a "circus elephant." I was enslaved to the world and still a believer in Jesus Christ. I was out partying, having fun, living a worldly life (not applying the benefits of my salvation). What if I found myself pregnant as a nineteen-year-old? No money, no education...I needed abortion to be "okay." So I created a God who believed life did not begin at conception. I made myself a god in my image, so I could live for nothing but myself and my ambitions. The Bible is clear about the result. Romans 1:21 says that your mind will be dark and confused. Worse yet, you will be living life with blinders on, and you will be a stranger to the one who created you and who is the lover of your soul. I cannot stress this enough—if you have lived a life broken by sin, and your mind is dark and confused, the God of heaven wants to love you and heal you. God did not write this scripture to condemn you, but to save you. (John 3:17)

In what ways, no matter how great or small, in the past or in the present, have you worshipped yourself?

_____

_____

_____

THE GREAT DEBATERS

"I will destroy human wisdom and discard their most brilliant ideas. So where does this leave the philosophers, the scholars, and the world's brilliant debaters? God has made them all look foolish and has shown their wisdom to be useless nonsense.

1 Corinthians 1:19–20 (NLT)

"O Lord, what great miracles you do, and how deep are your thoughts! Only an ignorant person would not know this! Only a fool would not understand.

Psalm 92:5–6 (NLT)

I have well-meaning, educated relatives who ask me things like, "How can you *not* believe in evolution?" "You *really* believe in a virgin birth?" "How can you believe people are not born gay?" The answer is simple and short; "I believe what God says." Period! Why would I believe what some professor teaches over what God says? Why would I choose a scientist's word over God's? These are just mere men. God is infallible. When I can go to the source of 100 percent rightness and truth all the time, why would I seek out truth from *people*? People are wrong all the time. Every day they stumble and fail. God is always right. He has never once stumbled. He has never failed.

I know this sounds way too simple. Guess what? It's because it is this simple. God is not complicated. You can search and study, learn difficult-to-pronounce theological terms and Greek translations, attend prestigious seminars on apologetics (which by the way, are really faith affirming and fascinating), but the truth is you can't *prove* there is a God any more than you can prove there isn't a God. God is everything. He is everywhere. He doesn't need to prove Himself. He's God. He wants you to believe in Him, even though it doesn't always make sense. He wants you to believe even though you can't see Him. Jesus even told his disciples the very same... "You believe because you have seen me. Blessed are those who haven't seen me and believe anyway" (John 20:29, NLT). He wants you to choose Him over the world, trust Him over trusting mere humans, and believe in Him even when you can't see Him.

We live in a world that wields doubt like a commodity. We find it endearing to doubt, like we are somehow more thoughtful and humble if we struggle with believing in all of God's truths. Confidence in God is not equated with arrogance. Confidence in God means that you don't have to spend your life wavering back and forth, falling for every popular belief of your day (2 Corinthians 11:3–4). Confidence in God means that you know beyond the shadow of a doubt you have been given an absolute, unchanging, perfected foundation in which to live a purposeful life, God's Word.

"I cried out, 'I'm slipping!' and your unfailing love supported me. When *doubts* filled my mind, your comfort gave me renewed hope and cheer" (Psalm 94:18–19).

In what ways, have you believed the media, your professors, or leading scientists? Some examples from my own life—parenting, politics, and marriage

_____

_____

_____

HOW DEEP ARE YOUR ROOTS?

And now just as you accepted Christ Jesus as your Lord, you must continue to live in obedience to him. Let your roots grow down deep into him and draw up nourishment from him, so you will grow in faith, strong, and vigorous in the truth you were taught. Let your lives overflow with thanksgiving for all he has done. Don't let anyone lead you astray with empty philosophy and high-sounding nonsense that come from human thinking and from the evil powers of this world, and not from Christ.

Colossians 2:6–8 (NLT)

I give these verses to every high school senior I teach, and I tell them to commit them to memory. Oh child of God, don't let people lead you astray. They trick you because the nonsense that comes out of their mouth is "high-sounding". In other words, they sound really intelligent. Their arguments make sense. They think people like you, who believe in what they would call myth and fairy-tale are ignorant fools, and they will tell you so. But don't be persuaded, for God says that they are the fool. Don't feel downtrodden. Jesus says, "Blessed are those who are persecuted because they believe in me, for the Kingdom of Heaven is theirs!" Matthew 5:10 (NLT)

Young believer or even old believer, you have been given the power of the living God. The power that parted the Red Sea, the power that tore down the walls of Jericho, the power that healed the sick, the power that created the universe, the power that crucified the sin of the world on a cross, and the power that raised the Son of Man three days later lives in you! Break free from your chains and don't be afraid to *want* God.

Have you been the believer from Jesus's parable of the Four Soils? "Other seed fell on shallow soil with underlying rock. The plant sprang up quickly, but it soon wilted beneath the hot sun and died because the roots had no nourishment in the shallow soil?" (Mark 4:5–6, NLT)

How deep are your roots? Are they shallow? Does God know you, but do you know Him? Really access yourself with a sincere heart.

_____

_____

My friend, you've been out alone in the desert too long. Come home. Believe. If God made you into a new creation when He saved you, then living the old ways with old beliefs is really not who you are. You're not being yourself. Embrace who you are and be yourself.

What if all of this sounds foreign to you? What if you are reading this and saying to yourself, "I've never even taken the first step." There is no time like the present. If you know the emptiness in your heart is because God is not there, tell him...right now. Tell Him you want to know Him, trust Him, and surrender to Him. Tell Him, even though it's still difficult to grasp, that you believe He allowed His Son, Jesus, to exchange His life for your sin. Tell Him you want to be new, pure, cleansed, and free. He'll do it...in an instant. Go ahead.

WEEK THREE

THE PRODUCT OF FAITH
STEP 2: "THEN YOUR FAITH WILL PRODUCE A LIFE OF MORAL EXCELLENCE."

What produces a life of moral excellence? *Faith!* What? Say it again. Out loud. Shout it. Get it through your head right now. *Faith! Faith! Faith!* The reason I am so emphatic about this is because so many—myself included—have unknowingly gotten this step wrong. God does not say to live a life of moral excellence and then He will make you faithful. No! He says to be faithful, and that faith and faith alone will begin to produce a life of moral excellence. He didn't say, "Obey my commandments and then love me." He said, "Love me," and then you will obey my commandments.

Yet faith can be so tricky for many of us. Faith is described in Hebrews 11:1 (NLT), "What is faith? It is the confident assurance that what we hope for is going to happen. It is the evidence of things we cannot yet see." This idea of believing in something we cannot *yet* see shows up again. Remember Jesus talked about it in John 20:29. It seems so simple, because it is so simple. King David defined it as this:

> The Lord protects those of child-like faith; I was facing death and then He saved me. Now I can rest again for the Lord has been so good to me. He has saved me from death, my eyes from tears, my feet from stumbling…And so I walk in the Lord's presence as I live here on earth.

> Psalm 116:6–9

God wants our child-like belief. Notice David's gratitude, he has seen all of God's goodness, and so he believes. He gives credit to where credit is due. If you know that the reason you're alive, the reason you are saved, the very reason you are breathing is thanks to God, it becomes more and more difficult to doubt Him. But to counter this—we have an enemy who is working tirelessly to derail our faith. His main goal is to deceive us and have us put our faith in all the wrong things.

Everybody has faith. It takes just a little faith to get out of bed in the morning. When you put your feet on the ground, you believe the ground will be beneath them. When you open your eyes, you believe you'll see the light of the sun. You believe when you turn on the shower that water will pour from the shower head. You believe that when you get into your car to drive to work that your place of employment will still be standing. Everybody has faith. God is just asking you to *give Him* a little more each day. Just believe a little more. If there is not enough money in your bank account to buy groceries, instead of immediately stressing out, say, "God, I am believing that somehow you will provide the money." Maybe God will give you an idea to make some extra cash, maybe you'll get a refund from your auto insurance company, maybe you'll get a bonus at work, maybe Aunt June thinks your birthday is this month instead of next month and she'll send you a little cash, or maybe God will speak to someone in your church about your financial woes and they will respond. Jesus says,

> So I tell you, don't worry about everyday life—whether you have enough food, drink, and clothes. Doesn't life consist of more than food and clothing? Look at the birds. They don't need to plant or harvest or put food in barns because your heavenly Father feeds them. And you are far more valuable to him than they are. Can all your worries add a single moment to your life? Of course not…Your heavenly Father already knows your needs, and he will give you all you need from day to day if you live for Him and make the Kingdom of God your primary concern.
>
> Matthew 6:25-27 and 32–33 (NLT)

When you actually give God faith, He gives faith back to you. Don't miss this. You give God your faith. You believe in something you can't yet see. Then when God acts, you see it. You see Him. And when you see Him, He gives you more faith. Now you believe a little more than you did yesterday. Now you trust God more for tomorrow, because of what you saw Him do today.

Our new business in home building was just a couple of years old when the economy collapsed and the banks all but shut down. On top of that, my oldest daughter had recently been diagnosed with asthma, and had a very expensive monthly medication that kept her breathing without episode. We were down to our last forty dollars. There was nowhere to go for any other funds. We were tapped. My husband called me from work and said that he needed $10,198.43 to cover payroll, rent, and pay ourselves. We had no prospects. Every client we had was more than a month away from closing with the banks, so we began to just walk in faith. I prayed without ceasing that God would supply our needs. My dear friend Julie called me out of the blue that same day and wanted to meet for dinner. I couldn't go to dinner because I couldn't pay for dinner. I asked instead if we could meet for coffee. I knew I could scrape together a dollar or two. As we began to talk, I felt led, even though I was a little embarrassed and a lot humbled to tell her about our financial situation. I explained that my daughter ran out of her medication tomorrow, and I had no idea how to pay for it. I also shared that if we didn't come up with the money our employees weren't getting a paycheck. I noticed she began texting someone with urgency. I asked who she was texting, and she replied, "Kyle." Kyle is her husband, who is also a doctor, who also had boxes of samples of the same medication that my daughter needed. *Bam!* God handled the first crisis! Then the next day, my husband called me from work and said, "Are you ready for this?

The bank just called and for some unforeseen reason they are moving up one of our client's closings to tomorrow. Guess how much our commission is? $10,200.00." I can just remember how grateful and awestruck I was by God. He was never going to let us fall! That client wasn't scheduled to close for five more weeks! God had done miracles for us! I am so humbled by His goodness.

Can you describe a time when you placed absolute trust in God to provide for any kind of situation?

_____

_____

How did He provide?

_____

_____

_____

Did you recognize God's activity in your situation and did you give Him thanks?

_____

Is there anything that you are worried about that you need to surrender to God?

_____

_____

CLEAN UP YOUR ACT ALREADY!

Now that you are transitioning from the truth that God will provide you with faith if you seek it, He will also—astonishingly enough—cover your sin too. That said, we humans find a way to bungle up His perfect ways with our own fruitless ideas. There is a long standing belief in the

Christian church that sin must supernaturally disappear from our lives the minute we believe. We think because now we are believers that *we* have to clean up our act. No more smoking, drinking too much, cussing, living with our boyfriend/girlfriend, etc. You're a Christian now! Act right! Straighten up! Let me give you an example. I used to work with a woman (we'll call her Tracy). Tracy was a recovering alcoholic and drug user. She had endured very traumatic and devastating abuse at the hands of the people who were supposed to love her the most. She now lived her life as a homosexual. We talked about God all the time. Honestly, because she brought it up almost every day. God was calling her. Tracy had so many questions and so many doubts, but her greatest concern was that if she accepted Christ's forgiveness, she would have to stop being a lesbian that very day. She would have to go home and tell her girlfriend that they were breaking up, and then she would find a new place to live. Now, can you guess who instilled this belief in her? You guessed it! Christians! Well-meaning Christians. Christians who still don't understand step two.

Upon my very first meeting with Tracy, she asked me bluntly, "Do you think I'm going to hell because I'm gay?" I replied, "No. No one goes to hell *because* they're gay. People go to hell because they reject the love and forgiveness of Jesus Christ."

What I wanted her to understand was that you don't have to worry about how to live a life of moral excellence. All you have to do is put your faith and trust in God. *He* will produce moral excellence in you. Think about it. I can't be godly without Him. It's only when I surrender who I am to Him that he begins to woo me. That loving courtship begins to convict, transform, and cultivate an extreme change in me.

Don't misunderstand me. I am not saying that obeying God is unimportant. In fact, it's vitally important if you want God's best.

> And how can we be sure we belong to Him? By obeying His commandments. If someone says, "I belong to God," but doesn't obey His commandments, that person is a liar and does not live in the truth. But those who obey God's word really do love Him. That is the way to know whether or not we live in Him.
>
> 1 John 2:3–5 (NLT)

Obedience to the Father is how we know we actually live in the truth. But we must make sure our obedience is coming from the right motives. Read the beginning of verse 5 again. "But those who obey God's word *really do love Him.*" Our obedience has to stem from faith and love and not from a societal, moral sensibility. Otherwise, we are just "tap dancing" to get to heaven, and we really never get to experience true and genuine communion with our God. I have firsthand experience with this, and it is a brutal existence.

In what ways do you think *you* have to clean up your own act?

_____

_____

THE BURDEN IS LIGHT

When I was in my early thirties, I was really struggling with my faith. I felt terrible about myself almost all the time. I was so burdened by "Christianity." I couldn't understand why I felt this way. I went to church regularly, read my Bible, taught Sunday school, prayed for people who were hurting. I loved the Lord. I really did. I wanted to grow and learn and know God. Why did my heart feel so heavy? I remember one day reading Jesus's words in Matthew 11:28–30 (NLT): "Come to me, all of you who are weary and carry heavy burdens, and I will give you rest. Take my yoke upon you. Let me teach you, because I am humble and gentle, and you will find rest for your souls. For my yoke fits perfectly, and the burden I give you is light." I remember thinking, *No it's not. Your burden is so heavy. I don't feel like my soul is at rest. What's wrong with me?*

The answer came through God's Word. In Romans 3:21–22 Paul writes,

> But now God has shown us a different way of being right in his sight—not by obeying the law but by the way promised in the Scriptures long ago. We are made right in God's sight when we trust in Jesus Christ to take away our sins. And we all can be saved in this same way, no matter who we are or what we have done.

Now skip down to verse 27 and 28,

> "Can we boast, then, that we have done anything to be accepted by God? No, because our acquittal

is not based on our good deeds. It is based on our faith. So we are made right with God through faith and not by obeying the law.

Okay, now skip to 31, "Well then, if we emphasize faith, does this mean that we can forget about the law? Of course not! In fact, *only when we have faith do we truly fulfill the law.*"

Check out Galatians 3:2–3

Let me ask you one question: Did you receive the Holy Spirit by keeping the law? Of course not, the Holy Spirit came upon you only after you believed the message you heard about Christ. Have you lost your senses? After starting your Christian lives in the Spirit, why are you now trying to become perfect by your own human effort?

Paul hit me right between the eyes! Had I lost my senses? I had. I wanted my sense restored. All I needed was to just believe in the words of my God. That's all I had to do. Just believe my God.

It was always right under my nose. I'd read these same verses many times before, but I don't think I really ever understood until that very moment. If it's by faith that I am saved and justified, then it is also by faith that I am sanctified! "Only when we have faith, do we truly fulfill the law." How did I miss this? I had a head-knowledge, but not a heart-knowledge. I was living by my deeds and not by my faith. God never said, "Be good and I will make you faithful." He said, "Be faithful and I will make you good."

We have to stop listening to the authorities of this world, because they don't have any authority over us! Those voices that tell us we're not good enough, not smart enough, not talented enough, not pretty enough, we don't serve enough, that we don't love enough…this is not God! When God speaks, He brings conviction, not shame. His conviction breeds love, ignites confidence, restores faith, brings unity, cultivates joy, and gives freedom.

Today, I try not to beat myself up. When I mess up, which is daily, I move on and move up. My faith has to come first. When I repent, instead of saying, "God, forgive me for…fill in the blank," I try to say, "God, I did it again. Give me the faith you need me to have to act like you." My will does not destroy the sin…faith is the *only* sin destroyer. Faith is the only way to a life of moral excellence.

Are you still walking with God into a life of moral excellence? Or are you seeing that this is where you might have chosen another path? Your path. It takes all of thirty seconds to make a change. Tell God. Tell Him you've been depending on yourself instead of Him. Tell Him that today you want to experience what it's like to *really* trust Him. Tell Him you want to see your faith growing in ways you never dreamed. Be watchful. Begin anticipating great things. You just invited God to be in control of your life. Congratulations!

Are you trying to be "good" or "faithful"?

———————————————————————

Are you feeling horrible about yourself because you don't think you're godly *enough*?

———————————————————————

Name the areas in your life in which you are struggling
with sin.

_____

_____

Now, ask God to give you the faith in Him that
you need, to be who He has created you to be. Don't be
discouraged that you're not perfect. Just be faithful.

WEEK FOUR

KNOWING GOD
STEP 3: "A LIFE OF MORAL EXCELLENCE LEADS TO KNOWING GOD BETTER"

HEARING HIS VOICE

It makes sense that a life lived in moral excellence leads to knowing God better, for so many reasons too. When I/you submit yourself to God's way, you say to Him, "I love you. I want what you want for me." This submission opens the door to God's voice. For example, when any or all of my four children are consistently obeying me, we're close. We're not wasting time dealing with rebellion and discipline. We're just living life together. They hear my words, they value my words, and our relationship is beautiful and peaceful because of that respect.

God is speaking; you just might not be listening. Or maybe you have been listening; you just didn't recognize His voice. Looking back on my walk with God, I recollect the many, many times God was speaking to me, but I just didn't realize it was Him. I began to recognize His life-altering voice when I surrendered everything to Him. Sadly, I was a believer for a long time before I allowed God to really take control of my life. He'd forgiven me, but now I was letting Him in, so He could begin perfecting me. When you begin to hear Him, you begin to *know* Him. "After he has gathered his own flock, he walks ahead of them, and they follow him because they recognize his voice" (John 10:4).

I remember being in my mid-twenties, and I would roll my eyes every time I heard a Christian say, "God told me," in part, because I wondered if people just said that to get their way, or they wanted to sound really religious, but mostly because of my own ignorance. I didn't know what I didn't know. I believed God's voice had to be this audible, earth-shattering, Moses and the burning bush kind of thing. Once again, I was making things so much harder than they were. Later, I began to see that God was gently speaking to me with kindness—through His Word, through His people, and through my own heart. Sure, I still have moments when I question, "Was that you, God? Or was it me? We all do, but in my ever evolving relationship with Him, He has granted me moments of such clarity that it just takes my breath away. Oh...how I love Him.

Do you recognize God's voice in your own life?

_____

Can you describe a time when you clearly heard God's voice in your life.

_____

_____

_____

KNOWING HIS MIND

When you choose to live morally, you begin to experience joy. I mean *real* joy. That's the kind of joy that surpasses your circumstances, the kind of joy that gives you peace, the kind of joy that gives you more faith. When you begin living with that kind of peace of mind, God's peace of mind, you stop noticing the world, and you start noticing God. Paul notes about his own journey with God in Galatians (6:14, NLT) "Because of that cross, my interest in the world died long ago, and the world's interest in me is also long dead." Not to mention, your life isn't nearly as drama ridden when you begin making moral choices. In First Thessalonians 4:11, we are told that our ambition should be to live a quieter life." A quiet life begins to sound really attractive when all *your* choices have only led to chaos. We need to make a very introspective decision that we don't need the world's attention anymore; we only want the attention of God. Craving the world's attention leads to a very anxious, desperate life.

Let's take for example the ripple effect. I'm sure you know someone who always seems to be in the throes of continuous drama (Maybe you are that someone). These folks tell anyone who will listen all about their many problems and how they just can't figure out how all these bad things happen to them. This is an example of a "world's attention" kind of day. Alarm clock goes off, there are two choices: get up or stay in bed. The chaos king or queen chooses to stay in bed. Now they are late for work, so they zoom down the road at the speed of light. Uh-oh...sirens. Now you have a ticket you can't afford to pay, and you're even later to work. As you can imagine, your boss is really ticked (as it happens, you're probably late a lot). He gives you a serious talking to. At this point, you can respond with respect and sincerity, or you can have a poor attitude, blaming everyone else for your terrible day and circumstances. Of course, you choose the latter. Now your boss is considering firing you over his lunch break, and you're off to the water cooler to gossip and complain about how nobody "gets you." Your day has been so trying that you feel like you need to blow off some steam. So instead of heading home to lick your wounds, you head to the local bar to get drunk and forget about the day. Now you're spending way too much on your bar tab with a credit card that is already charging you 24 percent interest, hanging out with people who don't make you better, and making decisions in your inebriated state that you will most assuredly live to regret. To make matters worse, you'll get home late if you get home at all, get a terrible night's sleep, have a horrible headache in the morning, and sleep through the alarm *again*. And the cycle continues over and over with a life spiraling more and more out of control.

If this is you, there is hope. The sin of living a chaotic life begins and ends with your desire for attention. People like attention. If they can be the center of someone's concern, prayer request, or conversation, they will. Who are we kidding? It's nice to be "important." Unfortunately, people who crave this addictively begin to live in chaos. They have to feed the opportunities that will captivate people's attention, even if it's the worst kind of attention. Truly the solution again is... practice. First you have to be broken enough to admit you can't live like this anymore, and then just like anything else, you have to desire change. This is where the practice begins. Your whole day is made up of choices. If you want to live a biblically "quiet," life blossoming with wisdom, maturity, prosperity, and peace, then you have to practice living that life. When the alarm clock goes off, get up, don't speed, be at work on time, work efficiently and cheerfully, go home, and eat a healthy dinner, go to an evening Bible study, have coffee with a friend (decaf, you have to get up tomorrow), pay with cash (you can afford the coffee, not the bar tab), go home, and go to bed. Start living this life for a week, asking God every day to fill you up with confidence so you don't need addictive, unhealthy affirmation from others. You'll be amazed at how your life will change. You'll start knowing God because now you can hear Him. It was way too noisy before.

When this edifying growth begins, the problems you do have in this world don't bother you nearly as much because you're not as concerned with *this* world. You are now more concerned with God's world. That's kingdom thinking, my friend. Now you're beginning to understand God's mind.

> But people who aren't Christians can't understand these truths from God's Spirit. It all sounds

foolish to them because only those who have the Spirit can understand what the Spirit means. We who have the Spirit understand these things, but others cannot understand us at all. How could they? For who can know what the Lord is thinking? Who can give Him counsel? But we can understand these things, *for we have the mind of Christ.*

1 Corinthians 2:14–16 (NLT)

When you allow the Holy Spirit to do His work, you actually begin to know the mind of God. Don't misunderstand me; His ways will always be higher than yours, and He may allow things in your life that just don't make any sense to you, but you handle it differently now. You know His mind, you know His heart for you, so trusting His decisions for your life becomes easier and easier.

Can you describe a time in your life when you were an attention junkie craving drama?

_____

_____

What kinds of practical applications can help us to know God's mind and desire God's attention above anyone else?

_____

_____

PURITY EQUALS DRAWING NEAR TO GOD

If you've been a believer for a while, and you've had a time where you wandered away because doing things your way sounded like more fun, this you'll understand. Sometimes, sin looks really appealing. Let's face the facts. Sin can be fun, at least for a while. As Craig Groeschel (pastor of Life Church) says, "Sin is like a big sneeze. It feels good coming out, but it leaves a big ole snotty mess."

> For you are a slave to whatever controls you. And when people escape from the wicked ways of the world by learning about our Lord and Savior Jesus Christ and then get tangled up with sin and become its slave again, they are worse off than before. It would be better if they had never known the right way to live than to know it and then reject the holy commandments that were given to them. They make these proverbs come true, "A dog returns to its vomit," and "A washed pig returns to the mud."
>
> 2 Peter 2:19b–22 (NLT)

See, God is perfect. He's holy, completely pure and without any blemish. He can't be around sin. That's why He traded your sin with His son's life. He wanted to be with you and to be in you. He wanted us to be one with Him. So when you live a life saturated in sin, *you* distance yourself from Him. Don't miss that. He doesn't walk away and create the distance. You do. You return to the vomit. You return to the mud, and God hates the loneliness you feel from the distance you create.

When we do something to someone we love that they hate, it creates distance. If your husband hates it when you're a nag, and you nag him regularly, it creates distance in your marriage. If you're child knowingly defies you, it creates distance. If your friend continually only talks and thinks about herself, it creates distance in the friendship. When we hurt God, sin against Him, it creates distance. God hates the loneliness we feel from the distance we create.

When my children were all babies, they would sit in their father's lap and he would snuggle them, hold them closely, and kiss them. Suddenly and without warning, Dad began to smell something atrocious. His precious little baby had made a very big stinky in his or her diaper. Now Dad is not holding the sweet baby closely. He has extended his arms, trying desperately to hand the child off to me (or any other person within in arm's length). Dad still loved his infant, but the smell of the dirty diaper caused him to hold the child at a distance.

Oh boy, how true this is. When we are walking with God, putting our faith in Him, loving Him, and spending time with Him, He has been able to cultivate in us a life of moral excellence; that clean and pure life that we are living leads to a deeper and more intimate relationship with Him. We actually truly begin to "know" God.

In contrast, the opposite is true. When we "make a stinky" and we habitually live in impurity, it becomes difficult to commune with God. Let's be honest; when we live in impurity, we aren't even interested in communing with God, and we withdraw ourselves from His presence. "Listen! The Lord is not too weak to save you, and he is not becoming deaf. He can hear you when you call. But there is a problem—your sins have cut you off from God…" (Isaiah 59:1–2b, NLT).

"Cling tight to your faith in Christ and always keep your conscience clear. For some people have deliberately violated their consciences: as a result their faith has been shipwrecked" (1 Timothy 1:19, NLT). Is your faith shipwrecked? God knows you're going to sin, but let's be clear—this is a heart issue. When you sin, but your heart aches over the sin, and you repent, and ask God to create in you a clean heart, and renew a right spirit within you, your faith is *not* shipwrecked. It's anything but. Your faith is winning the battle because your heart is desperately in love with God. But if your sin is deliberately habitual, and it overruns your life, and you aren't even thinking about what you're doing to yourself, your loved ones, your unloved ones, but most of all God, then you really are shipwrecked. David wrote a beautiful Psalm that speaks to the shipwrecked soul. Whether you're a shipwrecked believer or a shipwrecked unbeliever, let these words wash over you: Psalm 32 (NLT)

> Oh what a joy for those whose rebellion is forgiven, whose sin is put out of sight. What a joy for those whose record the Lord has cleared of sin, whose lives are lived in complete honesty! When I refused to confess my sin I was weak and miserable, and I groaned all day long. Day and night your hand of discipline was heavy on me. My strength evaporated like water in the summer heat. Finally, I confessed all my sin to you and stopped trying to hide them. I said to myself, "I

will confess my rebellion to the Lord." And you forgave me. All my guilt is gone. Therefore let all the godly confess their rebellion to you while there is still time, and they may not drown in the floodwaters of judgment. For you are my hiding place, you protect me from trouble. You surround me with songs of victory. The Lord says, 'I will guide you along the best pathway for your life. I will advise you and watch over you. Don't be like a senseless horse or mule that needs a bit and a bridle to keep it under control.' Many sorrows come to the wicked, but unfailing love surrounds those who trust in the Lord. So rejoice in the Lord and be glad, all you who obey Him! Shout for joy, all you whose hearts are pure!

Psalm 32 (NLT)

If we are dogs returning to the vomit of our old lives, how can we grow in God? Living a morally excellent life opens the door to God's voice. It truly is amazing to really hear God's voice, but hearing Him regularly cannot be accomplished without a heart that is craving faith and obedience.

Are you habitually "making stinkies" that distance you from God?

_____

Is there unconfessed sin in your life that is crippling your relationship with God? Is your faith shipwrecked?

_____

Can you describe a time in your life when you distanced yourself from God by your sin?

_____
_____
_____

I urge you to follow David's example. Confess your rebellion and grant God what He wants...the faith in Him to change your heart and cleanse your soul.

DON'T UNDERESTIMATE YOUR ENEMY

You have an enemy and his name is Satan, the devil, Lucifer, Beelzebub—call him whatever you want. He's real, and he wants to derail you from truth and freedom. He wants you to return to the mud and the vomit. His objective is to seek you out and destroy you. He will use whatever ammunition he can wield against you. He will use your pride, your shame, your intelligence, your low self-esteem, your jealousy, your anger, your insecurity; and you won't even know what hit you. Remember how I fell into a system of trusting my deeds, instead of trusting my God? This is where it happened for me. I became overcome with being "good." Don't think for a second that Satan wasn't cheering that problem on. He loved it. He wanted me to believe that my faith was a burden too heavy to carry. His seductions are so finessed that we can easily be manipulated by them if we are not armed and alert. In the second book of Corinthians chapter 11 verse 14, it is stated, "Satan is disguised as an angel of light." This is why staying in close communion with the Father is so vital. I was fooled for a while, but I was steadfast in my relationship with Him. I didn't walk away, and I allowed Him to carry me through. He revealed the truth to me. We have to know *what* the truth is so we can protect ourselves from the lie.

The truth is you are who God says you are. You've done bad things, but *you* are not bad. You are forgiven and holy. You are set apart. You are not your past. That's all been wiped clean. Now as John Eldredge said so perfectly in his book, *Love and War*, "Stop making agreements with the enemy and make agreements with God." In other words, every time we believe that we're shameful, that we're controlled by our urges, that we are not good enough, or even that we are too smart for God; realize that you are agreeing with the enemy of your soul and therefore disagreeing with God. But when we believe the Word of God and put into action the truth of who we are *in* God, we are agreeing with God instead of arguing with Him. Scripture says that we cannot defeat the devil's stronghold on our lives with human effort.

> We are human, but we don't wage war with human plans and methods. We use God's mighty weapons, not mere worldly weapons, to knock down the Devil's strongholds. With these weapons we break down every proud argument that keeps people from knowing God. With these weapons we conquer their rebellious ideas, and we teach them to obey Christ.
>
> 2 Corinthians 10:3–5 (NLT)

> Put on all your armor so that you will be able to
> stand firm against all the strategies and tricks of
> the Devil. For we are not fighting against people
> made of flesh and blood, but against the evil
> rulers and authorities of the unseen world.
>
> Ephesians 6:11–12 (NLT)

Enemy Says	God Says
Your marriage is destined to fail.	Genesis 2:24
You're a horrible mother and you'll never be able to control your temper.	Proverbs 31:26
Your child's illness is crippling.	Jeremiah 30:17
You're not good enough, smart enough, pretty enough.	1 Peter 3:3–4

Even if you think you have screwed things up so badly that there is no hope, God answers that proclamation with a resounding, "*No!*" Psalm 145:14 (NLT) says, "The Lord helps the fallen and lifts up those beneath their loads." It goes on to say in verses 18–19, "The Lord is close to all who call on Him sincerely. He fulfills the desires of those who fear Him. He hears their cries for help and rescues them." Think of your life as a football field, and every time you agree with the enemy, he pushes you back, but every time you agree with God, you push back the enemy and begin to dominate the field. Your goal is to push him back into your own end zone. James 4:7 (NLT) says, "Resist the devil and he will flee from you." You resist the enemy by being in agreement with God.

David wrote in Psalms 44:5–7 (NLT),

Only by Your power can we *push back* our enemies; only in your name can we trample our foes. I do not trust my bow; I do not count on my sword to save me; it is You who gives us victory over our enemies; it is You who humbles those who hate us.

While David might have been referring to a human enemy, our greatest enemy is the one who Job 2:1 calls the Accuser. Think about that name, the Accuser. Who is that voice that accuses you and causes you to feel ashamed, filthy, worthless? It's the one who is called the Accuser.

Are you trying to repair a broken marriage with a Dr. Phil book? I have nothing against Dr. Phil, but his methods will not defeat the destroyer of your soul. Are you trying to beat depression with "just" medication? Nothing against medication, but have you asked God to heal your mind and your heart? Are you trying to beat alcoholism by sheer will alone? Are you trying to conquer fear, pride, jealousy, pornography, sexual promiscuity, bitterness, rage, etc. all by yourself? I hope not. You need God. You need His power. You need His strength. Your enemy is stronger than you, but he can't hold a candle to the one true God who lives inside you. "Greater is He that is in you, than he that is in the world" (1 John 4:4).

Maybe right now you're thinking, *Yeah, I've tried prayer before, but I'm not sold. I don't really believe that God is going to act.* Once again, there are multiple stories that depict a God who answers the prayers of His children, but let me just give you two examples.

In Daniel chapter 10, our hero Daniel has already been delivered from the lion's den. In chapter 7, God begins revealing to Daniel visions of future events. In chapter 9, Daniel commences to humbly fast and pray without ceasing asking for mercy and forgiveness for his people. In chapter 10, God sends words of great encouragement to Daniel, but more importantly to us.

> Just then a hand touched me and lifted me, still trembling, to my hands and knees. And the man said to me, 'Oh Daniel, greatly loved of God, listen carefully to what I have to say to you. Stand up, for I have been sent to you.' When he said this to me, I stood up, still trembling with fear. Then he said, 'Don't be afraid, Daniel. Since the first day you began to pray for understanding and to humble yourself before your God, your request has been heard in Heaven. I have come to answer your prayer.
>
> Daniel 10:10–12

Wow! Daniel prayed humbly and passionately, and God heard him immediately, and then God answered his request. God is on the throne, and He hears your cries and dispatches help with immediacy. Are you praying humbly, sincerely, passionately? Notice that Daniel had to be lifted to his hands and knees, which can only mean he was flat on his face, pleading to God. That's passion. That's humility. That's sincerity.

> Are there strongholds in your life deceiving you into believing your enemy instead of your God?
>
> _____
>
> _____

Are you using spiritual weapons to defeat your enemy?

_____

How can you implement spiritual warfare into your life to gain victory over your strongholds?

_____

_____

THE IMPORTANCE OF BEING EARNEST

How do you pray? James 5:16b says, "The earnest prayer of a righteous person has great power and wonderful results." Do you really believe God can and will break Satan's strongholds in your life, or do you just half-heartedly go through the motions never really expecting God to do great things? Daniel knew God could and would deliver, and his belief was demonstrated by the manner in which he prayed.

In Mark chapter 5, there is a woman who, as the Bible describes, had been hemorrhaging for twelve years. Can you imagine? Twelve years with no cure or help in sight until the day that Jesus walked through her town. A huge crowd surrounded Him, and the disciples were trying to help him navigate through the crowd. It must have looked like Justin Bieber trying to walk down the hallway of an all-girl middle school.

> She had heard about Jesus, so she came up behind him through the crowd and touched the fringe of his robe. For she thought to herself, 'If I can just touch his clothing, I will be healed.' Immediately the bleeding stopped, and she could

feel that she had been healed! Jesus realized at once that healing power had gone out from him, so he turned around in the crowd and asked, 'Who touched my clothes?' His disciples said to him, 'All this crowd is pressing around you. How can you ask, 'Who touched me?' But he kept on looking around to see who had done it. Then the frightened woman, trembling at the realization of what had happened to her, came and fell at his feet and told him what she had done. And he said to her, 'Daughter, your faith has made you well. Go in peace. You have been healed.'

Mark 5:27–34 (NLT)

Can I just say, wow, wow, wow! Can you picture this woman in your mind? She must have gotten down on her hands and knees and crawled through the dirt and dust, people were probably shoving her around and stepping on her fingers, but she had to get to the one who would save her. She believed in His power. She knew that He could transform her. She thought, *If I can just touch the fringe of His robe…just the fringe of His robe.* She was willing to look stupid, to get knocked around a bit, to humble herself, to be a little embarrassed because she *knew* Jesus was that powerful. This power is readily available to heal you, your hurt, your wounds, your sickness, your addiction. Can you look stupid, get knocked around a bit, risk a little embarrassment, humble yourself…to be healed? To be saved? To be rocked by God's power?

Do you *really* believe God is who He says He is? Do you believe He is more powerful than any problem you have? Do you trust that he can conquer any problem in your life, and are you willing to step out on a limb like the lady from the book of Mark? Are you willing to be perceived as weak, so you can be strong (2 Corinthians 12:8–10)?

By now, maybe you have seen the fork in the road where at some point in your walk with God, you detoured. Has your faith been shipwrecked? I wish I could say that my faith has been unwavering, that I hadn't ever walked away from God to do things my way. Truth is, I have walked away more times than I would like to own up to. The beauty of God is that His mercy is unfailing. His mercies truly are new every morning. If you detoured, get back on the road to victory. So many believers never get to experience the fullness of everything God is, because they've already jumped ship by now, and their enemy convinces them to be resigned to a life alone at sea without a life jacket. Where are you? Are you still on the road to genuine godliness?

Let's try something—pray earnestly over your stronghold. You might need to get on your knees, you might even need to get on your face, speak out your passionate, earnest prayer to God. He will hear you with immediacy. Trust that even if the problem still exists tomorrow, that God has dispatched help, and in His time, and in His perfect will, your prayer is being answered. Write down your experience.

_____

_____

_____

WEEK FIVE

SELF-CONTROL
STEP 4: "KNOWING GOD BETTER LEADS TO SELF-CONTROL"

I asked my class to describe a person that has developed self-control. They said things like, "they can withstand temptation" and "they're not driven by their emotions." Pretty good answers. Scripture says it best, as a person who is *controlled* by the Holy Spirit.

> Don't act thoughtlessly, but try to understand what the Lord wants you to do. Don't be drunk with wine, because that will ruin your life. Instead, let the *Holy Spirit fill and control you.* Then you will sing psalms and hymns and spiritual songs among yourselves, making music to the Lord in your hearts. And you will always give thanks for everything to God the Father in the name of our Lord Jesus Christ.
>
> Ephesians 5:17–20 (NLT)

Well, what does it mean to be controlled by the Holy Spirit? First, let's try our best to give it a definition. For those of you who are thinking, *I'm really not sure how to draw a perfect picture of the Holy Spirit*, well, join the club of millions of other Christians. While the Bible gives us a beautiful illustration of what the Holy Spirit is, it is far too mystical and supernatural for us humans to completely understand. God's thinking is so much higher than ours that we will never understand all the nuances of the Holy Spirit this side of heaven.

But to put it simply, the Holy Spirit is God *in* you. See, God wanted us to be one with Him. But we couldn't, because we were sinful, and God can't be a part of sin, because he is perfect and pure. So He sent His Son, Jesus—who was fully God and fully man—to earth to die for our sin. Your sin, along with the rest of the world's sin, was hung on Him as He suffered and died on the cross; and when He died, so died the sin of the world. "He canceled the record that contained the charges against us. He took it and destroyed it by nailing it to Christ's cross" (Colossians 2:14, NLT). So when you ask God to forgive you of your sin, by accepting and believing that His son died for your sin, then your sin is forgiven forever—once and for all time (Hebrews 9:12). At that moment, the Holy Spirit literally enters your body, and you are made one with God (See Acts chapter 2). I have to stop for a minute. As I'm writing this, I am just in awe of God. Not only was He willing to forgive me; He allowed his perfect son to die for me, and then He actually wanted to live *in* me. I've been a believer for many years, and this still just blows my mind. God is, as always, radically generous! He also gives us an extensive description of the Holy Spirit in His Word to help us better understand the awesomeness inside us.

The Holy Spirit...

- Helps us know God's thoughts (1 Corinthians 2:15–16)
- Imparts glory to each believer (2 Corinthians 3:18)
- Has placed eternity in us now (2 Corinthians 5:5)
- Makes us new creations (2 Corinthians 5:17)
- Sin always tries to push Him out (Galatians 5:17)
- Produces spiritual fruit in us (Galatians 5:22–23)
- Our guarantee that God will keep His promises (Ephesians 1:13–14)
- Brings unity to believers (Ephesians 4:3)
- Carries out God's work in us (Philippians 1:6)
- Power transforms us (1 Thessalonians 1:5)
- Helps us to discern false teaching (1 John 2:26–27)
- Gives us strength for extraordinary tasks (Judges 3:10)
- Helps us speak for Christ (Matthew 10:19–20)
- Cannot be taken from you (Matthew 10:29–31)
- Makes our reform last (Luke 11:24–26)
- Helps us to understand the Bible (Luke 24:45)
- Helps us worship (John 4:21–24)
- Urges us towards salvation (John 6:44)
- Brings deep and lasting peace (John 14:27)
- Prerequisite for Christian service (Acts 6:8–10)
- Guides us away from wrong places (Acts 16:7–9)
- Helps us pray (Romans 8:26-27)
- Gives us the power to live a Christian life (Romans 8:2)

> Jesus replied, 'The truth is no one can enter the Kingdom of God without being born of water and the Spirit. Humans can reproduce only human life, but the Holy Spirit gives new life from Heaven. So don't be surprised at my statement that you must be born again. Just as you can hear the wind but can't tell where it comes from or where it is going, so you can't explain how people are born of the Spirit.
>
> John 3:5–8 (NLT)

> I have given them the glory you gave me, so that they may be one, as we are—I in them and you in me, all being perfected into one.
>
> John 17:22–23

I don't know *how* the Holy Spirit enters us, but I know He does. He is in me. He gives me peace that passes all understanding, strength for tomorrow, and power for today. But most of all, love. Love for Him, love for others, and love for myself. Thank you, Jesus.

When you read the bullets describing the Holy Spirit, was there one description in particular that really made your heart leap? Explain.

_____

_____

HANDING OVER CONTROL

Now, how do we live a life controlled by the Holy Spirit? The Bible is clear that just because He lives in us, doesn't mean we are now perfect people subject to no temptation.

I wish, but we spend our lives learning to submit ourselves to His control in order to *have* self-control.

> But when the Holy Spirit controls our lives, he will produce this kind of fruit in us: love, joy, peace, patience, kindness, goodness, faithfulness, gentleness, and *self-control.* Here there is no conflict with the law. Those who belong to Christ Jesus have nailed the passions and desires of their sinful nature to his cross and crucified them there. If we are living now by the Holy Spirit, let us follow the Holy Spirit's leading in every part of our lives.
>
> Galatians 5:22–25 (NLT)

Let's not be deceived. Christians sin all the time. Sometimes they lead a life so saturated in sin that you would never even know they were believers in Christ. Galatians 5:16-17 depicts a person who is saved, but must make a choice everyday.

> So I advise you to live according to your new life in the Holy Spirit. Then you won't be doing what your sinful nature craves. The old sinful nature loves to do evil, which is just opposite from what the Holy Spirit wants. And the Spirit gives us desires that are opposite from what the sinful nature desires. These two forces are constantly fighting each other, and your choices are never free from this conflict.

Yes. You will still sin. But the more you choose the desires of the Spirit nature, you will begin to sin less and less. It's impossible not to (John 3:31, "He must become greater and greater and I must become less and less").

Say you have two potted plants, and one is Spirit and the other is sin. What happens to the plant I feed and water and nourish? It grows. In contrast, what happens to the plant I starve? It withers and dies. If you feed the sin plant, you can be assured that God will never leave you. "I give them eternal life, and they will never perish. No one will snatch them away from me" (John 10:28, NLT). You will become desensitized to your sin, and His voice will become fainter and fainter in your life. If you feed the Spirit plant, God begins to flourish in your heart, and your actions follow suit. The sin plant is starved, and it begins to wither. The more you feed the Spirit, the less presence and influence sin has in your life. The beauty of this is that the power of God is so overwhelming, He makes it difficult to ignore Him for long. God wins. He's God. What did you expect?

Which plant are you nourishing right now?

_____

Can you describe a time in your life when you were starving the Spirit and what was the outcome?

_____

_____

What event or circumstance did God use to draw you back to Him?

_____

_____

In what ways do you see yourself being transformed by the Holy Spirit? (reference the Holy Spirit's description on page 75)

_____

_____

YOUR MOUTH

How can I know the sins lurking in my heart? Cleanse me from these hidden faults. Keep me from deliberate sins. Don't let them control me. Then I will be free of guilt and innocent of great sin. May the *words of my mouth* and the meditations of my heart be pleasing to you, O Lord, my Rock and my Redeemer.

Psalms 19:12–14 (NLT)

And the tongue is a flame of fire. It is full of wickedness that can ruin your whole life. It can turn the entire course of your life into a blazing flame of destruction, for it is set on fire by hell itself.

James 3:6 (NLT)

Yikes! That's powerful. Do you gossip? Do you use foul and vulgar language? Do you lie? Do you give into your anger and spew forth rage? Yeah, we all have. You are not alone. Wow, when I think about my mouth twenty years ago. I could cause a fleet of sailors to blush, and I could lie so well I should have been recruited by the CIA.

Ten years ago, I was a woman of God. I chose God every day, but I still had problems with rage and gossip.

I would convince myself *my* gossip was righteous. Years ago, there were some serious problems brewing at my church. I found a person, another godly woman, who felt the same way I did, and we gossiped. Boy, did we gossip. We only said these things to each other—that's okay, right? Wrong. We needed to vent—nothing wrong with that, right? Wrong again. The problems needed to be exposed, so it was necessary that we talk about it, right? Oh, so wrong. It only took a couple of months for God to convict us both so heavily that we mutually agreed to never speak of these things again. From that time on, I have tried very diligently to keep my mouth shut. Do I say things on occasion that I shouldn't? Yeah, of course I do. But I live under the control of the Spirit, and so the habit of gossip is dead in me.

Rage—I don't even like to talk about this one, but here it goes. I am a recovering rage-aholic. Hell hath no fury like mine, when I lose control of my anger. It was over ten years ago and I was a wife and a mother of two, and desperately trying to hide my nasty temper from the world. I begged God to change me, make me patient, make me gentle, make me kind. Why didn't he just sprinkle magical God dust on me, and I would have the temperament of Snow White? The answer to my prayers came with a strange and puzzling arrival. Leave it to God to do things His way. My husband and I were done having children, and—surprise, surprise—I discovered I was pregnant. "God, why? Why would you give me another child? I'm a terrible mother! Why?" These were my secret prayers. That precious child came and five months later, I discovered I was pregnant again!

That would put these two new babies fourteen months apart! "God, No! No! No! What are you doing? I can't do this! I don't have it in me!" Little did I know that God had it in Him. Six months after my fourth child was born, I noticed I didn't lose my cool like I had in the past. I had more patience. I was gentler, kinder. God created a situation in which I leaned completely on Him. I didn't have any other choice. I gave Him everything. He took everything, and He cultivated something beautiful in me. I'm not going to tell you that since that time I have never once lost my temper. I have, but it's not a habit. God is giving me self-control.

Is your mouth under the control of the Holy Spirit?

What is a sure fire way to begin to control your tongue?

Can you describe how God has worked in you to give Him control over your mouth?

YOUR MIND

It is the thought life that defiles you. For from within, out of a person's heart, come evil thoughts, sexual immorality, theft, murder, greed, adultery, wickedness, deceit, eagerness for lustful pleasure, envy, slander, pride, and foolishness.

Mark 7:20–22 (NLT)

Oh boy, can our minds lead us astray. From thoughts of lust, paranoia, worry, negativity, plotting wickedness, guilt and shame, or even thinking too much of our own intelligence, we get ourselves into trouble. Contrary to popular, worldly belief, you actually can control your thoughts.

> Fix your thoughts on what is true and honorable and right. Think about things that are pure and lovely and admirable. Think about things that are excellent and worth of praise. Keep putting into practice all you learned from me and heard from me and saw me doing, and the God of peace be with you.
>
> Philippians 4:8–9 (NLT)

Paul was speaking to the church in Philippi when he used the key word *practice*. It takes practice to take your thoughts captive. How many times a day does your mind wander to a place that is the opposite of what these verses describe? Our minds can be used as powerful instruments of God's goodness if we surrender ourselves to Him. Romans 12:2 says, "Don't copy the behavior and customs of this world, but let God transform you into a new person by changing the way you *think*."

Do you think negatively? "I'll never be able to change." "Trying to heal this relationship is a losing battle." "I don't have what it takes to make a difference." "My past is so ugly, God can't use me." "I'm a loser." That's your sin nature, friend. Your enemy wants you to make these agreements with him. He wants you to resign yourself to that thought pattern. No. Agree with God. He can transform, He can heal, He can make a difference, He can forgive, He says you are victorious. Scripture says He can change the way you think. Have you asked Him? Do it right now.

I'll be honest with you. Allowing God to do this work in me has been the most exhausting He has ever done. I asked Him this: "God, whenever my thoughts wander off to something that is not of you...whatever it might be—bitterness, negativity, worry, paranoia, lust, shame, whatever—redirect me. Catch me and remind me to change my thought patterns." Guess what? He did. I couldn't believe how often I drifted into unhealthy thoughts. And *bam!* God said, "Pray." I prayed, "God, redirect me, control me." I literally would do this twenty-five to thirty times a day. Now, it's second nature. I put it into *practice*. Once again, if you think that today I never have an ugly thought...think again. I'm human and so are you, but I'm on the mend. Paul writes to the Philippians,

> I don't mean to say that I have already achieved these things or that I have already reached perfection! But I keep working toward the day when I will finally be all that Christ Jesus saved me for and wants me to be. No dear brothers and sisters, I am still not all I should be, but I am focusing all my energies on this one thing: Forgetting the past and looking to what lies ahead.
>
> Philippians 3:12–13 (NLT)

Listen, you're going to fail. But how are you going to respond to that failure? Paul says, "Forget the past and look to what lies ahead." When you fail, repent quickly. Don't give the enemy any ground. Forgive yourself and start again."

Are you struggling with stinkin' thinkin'?

_____

What kinds of victory are you depriving yourself from because of negative thinking?

_____

How can you begin to take your thoughts captive this week?

_____

_____

How do you respond to your failures? Do you linger in them, or do you repent quickly and move forward?

_____

_____

YOUR BODY

Is God in control of your body? Is He in control of the places you allow your body to be? Is He in control of the things you do with your body? Is He in control of the substances you put into your body? Your body is the temple of the living God. Did you get that? God lives in your body. Not figuratively. Not symbolically. Literally. Your body and the Holy Spirit are one. What you do to your body you also do to the Spirit of God. So when you defile your body, you defile God (see 1 Corinthians 6:12–20).

When I was in college, I hung with bad company. Actually, if I'm being honest, I *was* bad company. We went to, as my teenage children would call it, very "skanky" bars. I would drink way too much and smoke and curse and say all kinds of vulgar things. Men would look at me, and I knew exactly what was on their minds. All the while, I was a believer. I was feeding the "sin plant," but I was a believer. God was still in me. When I would go to these places, and I'm not kidding about this, I felt an actual heaviness on my chest, like someone just laid a twenty pound weight on my chest. I began to hear an inner voice, and at the time, I didn't understand that it was God's voice. It said, "Get out of here. This is not where you are supposed to be. You're better." Sadly, it would be a period of time before I actually obeyed, but the Holy Spirit was talking to me. He was trying to get the body that was shared with Him out of a sinful and perverse place.

THE S WORD

I'll be honest; I don't even like to talk about sex. Not because it makes me feel uncomfortable, but because it's all anyone in our society ever wants to talk about, look at, hear about, and experience. See, here's the deal. The devil is currently manipulating us into believing what the world believes about sex, and it makes me so angry because sex doesn't belong to the world. It's God's. He created it. It's His baby. He knows *everything* about sex; more than the guys in the locker room, more than Oprah, more than any leading sex therapist. He is the *true* expert. So when He says, "These are the perimeters for healthy sex," why don't we listen? We wouldn't go to a baker to repair our car, and we wouldn't go to a mechanic to buy cupcakes for our child's birthday, so why would we go to the world for the lowdown on sex? Sex outside God's guidelines is not just about the easy, in your face consequences that we all know about—pregnancy, disease, emotional baggage, tarnished reputations, self-loathing. As if all those painful results weren't enough, sex outside of God's guidelines has far more reaching repercussions than most people—myself included—ever expect or realize.

Let's be clear. When I say "sex," I don't just mean the act of sex. What do you let your eyes see? What do you let your ears hear? God says to run from sexual temptation. Not walk, *run* (1 Corinthians 6:18). Staying away from any media, Facebook pages, places, people, or situations that could tempt you is key. When my husband was in college, he was fortunate to build friendships with a group of really godly young men. They were committed to staying pure. There were evidently multitudes of beautiful women on campus, and some of the guys were really struggling. In order to nip their temptation in the bud, they agreed that when they walked on campus from class to class, they would look down at the sidewalk instead of the tanned legged scenery. Looking was causing them to be tempted, so they stopped looking. They didn't look where they didn't want to go. If you don't want to destroy your family by having an affair with your high school boyfriend, then ignore his Facebook friend request. If you don't want to have a worldly view of sex, then stop watching *Sex in the City* reruns. Don't look where you don't want to go.

UNFORESEEN CONSEQUENCES

Keeping your body pure from sexual acts outside God's will keeps you from an array of negative consequences. Craig Groeschel illustrates this point in *Love, Sex, and Happily Ever After*. He wrote that he and his wife remained sexually pure until their wedding night. Before he was a believer, he had "been around the block," but when he met his future wife, Amy, they maintained their purity. They have been married for over twenty years now, and he never doubts her faithfulness. Why? Because when they were dating, she was able to control her body. If she could control her body while they were dating, then that gave him great assurance that she could and would control her body as a married woman. That is a security of staying pure that most people—including myself—don't even consider. How much do you want to trust your spouse? My guess is that you want to trust him or her absolutely and completely. Purity before marriage contributes to that security.

What if you are completely infatuated with someone and you engage in a sexual relationship only to realize months later that he really isn't the right one for you? The world would have you believe sex is just recreational, but God says it unites two bodies into one, that includes your spirits, your minds, and your souls. Now you feel extremely tied to this person; as you should, but your relationship is based on attraction and sex, and not on a Christ-centered deep love and respect for one another. You know in your heart of hearts that he is not the one, but because you have prematurely entered into a physical relationship, you just can't let go. More pain, more poor decisions to follow...

Or how about this one: have you considered your future children will one day ask you about your experience with sex? They will want to know all about your love story with your spouse. Do you want to share your story with pride? Or will you want to lie, because the truth is too dark to share with your precious, innocent children? Sex, God's way, protects you from all of this future conflict and pain. His way provides love, intimacy, security, and joy. The world's way desensitizes us and makes us numb in order for us to survive the pain of those decisions.

Listen, don't get all bent out of shape if your courting story was less than perfect. Let's not forget who our God is. God forgives *all* sin. God renews and transforms His children. If you are caught up in hidden sexual sin, then repent. Our God is a God of purity and renewal. Put faith into your God who wants only good for you.

YOU ARE WHAT YOU EAT

What about drugs, alcohol, and—here is the one I want to focus on—food? I in no way want to downplay the horrible impact chemical addiction has on our lives, but we are living in a country where more and more people are overweight and even obese. I'm not an expert, but I would venture a guess that food is slowly killing more people than drugs or alcohol. Yet, our society doesn't want to acknowledge overeating as sin. This is very close to my heart, because I have struggled with my weight for twenty-five years. In the last twenty years, I had gained one hundred pounds. Wow, as I was typing that number, I can't even believe it myself. Here is the crazy thing: I have been on a "diet" for most of those two decades.

Recently, I decided enough was enough. I was a woman who *seemed* to live a life controlled by the Holy Spirit, but this was one vice that I wouldn't give to God. I believed my enemy. I made all kinds of agreements with him. I'd say to myself, "This mountain is too high, I just can't do it." All the while the thriving confidence God wanted for me was hanging on by a thread. I was defeated, insecure, unhealthy, and feeling very unattractive in my own skin. I wasn't living my life with boldness because I was fat. Instead of being excited to take my kids to an amusement park, I feared it. What if I didn't fit in the ride? I didn't walk into a room with my shoulders back and my head held high. I was living in timidity. The seventh verse of 2nd Timothy chapter 1 took on a whole new meaning for me. "For God has not given us a spirit of fear and timidity, but of power, love, and *self-discipline*." My dear friend Shannon said to me, "Sarena, this is so much bigger than food. This is a spiritual problem." She didn't tell me the popular reasons for overeating. She didn't say that it stemmed from past hurts or stress. She said I was filling myself up with food instead of God. I was giving my life, in so many ways, to the destroyer. I was giving up on God's best for me by giving my enemy ground.

I decided, "No more!" This time I meant it. I wanted to do things the right way. No more starving and binging. I called an endocrinologist I knew, and set up an appointment. They gave me a complete health "work up." They did it all, took blood, urine, they even gave me a weird breathalyzer test to check my metabolism. Was I already insulin resistant? Was my cholesterol through the roof? Turns out, God was gracious to me. My health was relatively good, but my Spirit was not. They put me on a healthy and reasonable weight loss plan. It's been six months now, and I have lost thirty-three pounds. I'm not setting any records, or shedding weight like the contestants on *The Biggest Loser*, but that is not what it's about for me. I am in the process of relinquishing control to my God. It's slow and steady, and God is transforming my mind and my body. Every day, I am gaining the confidence God wants me to have. God is increasing, and I am decreasing (no pun intended). What's interesting about self-control is that you actually have to give up *your* control first. When I am tempted, I say to myself, "God's plan for you is so much bigger than that bag of potato chips." God's plan for you is so much bigger than _____. Fill in the blank. Whatever it is that keeps you from experiencing the abundance God wants for you, give up your control. Go ahead, push the enemy back and let God flex His all powerful muscles in your life. God is victorious. He always wins.

When you have setbacks, don't be discouraged. Remember, we're human; we fail. But don't give Satan your ear when it happens. He will try to convince you to feel shame and defeat. Don't agree with him. Agree with God. You are His masterpiece, you are valued, you are chosen, you are precious, you are loved. Repent quickly, and, with immediacy, get back on the road to true godliness.

Do any of these physical issues resonate with you? Sex, food, eating disorders, alcohol, drugs, allowing your body to be in the wrong places. What can you begin doing today to give God control over your body?

_____

_____

I spent so much time on this chapter because this is where so many walk away. Living a life controlled by the Holy Spirit takes a little more discipline, a little more prayer, a little more surrendering, a little more vulnerability, and a little more dying to yourself. If you live this way, you'll stand out a little more, you might even be considered "weird" by worldly standards. Wear it as a badge of honor. People might belittle you, but secretly they'll respect you, and they will want what you have.

WEEK SIX

PATIENT ENDURANCE
STEP 5: "SELF-CONTROL LEADS TO PATIENT ENDURANCE"

So first we make every effort to apply the benefits of our salvation, then our faith will produce a life of moral excellence, then we begin to truly know God, then God begins to develop in us self-control, and then that self-control leads us to patient endurance.

First, what exactly *is* patient endurance? Actually, before we get to that—what is patience? When I asked this question in my high school class, the consensus was this: "the ability to wait with grace." Waiting is not my strong suit. But over the years, God has been transforming me into a waiting believer. Waiting on God's timing, waiting on God's direction, waiting on God's best.

In the 90s my husband, Bob and I owned a business in the technology industry. Our business had thrived in years past, but the technology crash in 2000 had left us with a business that was just barely making ends meet. We began praying for God's direction. In a matter of months, he led us to the conclusion that it was time to move on and close our doors. We could have kept the doors open for another year or so, but God was telling us to move on now. We had no idea what our next career would be, but we decided to step out in faith believing that God would provide. When I would tell people what we were doing, they would ask with concerned eyes and voices, "What are you guys going to do?" I said with a smile, "I don't know." Their concerned faces turned to terrified faces. If *my* friend told me that, I would have reacted the same way. God was granting us His peace. There was no other explanation. We had saved some money to prepare for this day, but for the long term, we didn't have a clue. God replaced anxiety with assurance.

I had always wanted to try my hand at real estate. I decided to go to school. That took a week. I got my license and started combing the real estate pages for fixer-uppers. Bob was fairly handy, so we thought we would try to "flip" a house. We bought a really beat-up little two-bedroom house that I thought had oodles of potential. It had original wood floors and kitchen cabinetry. It was darling with so much character. We converted the garage, replaced the electrical, the plumbing, repaired the roof, new tile, new fixtures, fresh paint, and—*presto chango*—it was adorable. Before we had even finished that house, another one had come available in a fantastic school district, and then another. Before you knew it, we were making a living flipping houses. My husband was enjoying the physical labor after years in the corporate world. He was using so many of the skills he had learned as a young man, roofing houses and laying concrete, but he was also enjoying all of the new skills he was learning from some of the subcontractors we had hired along the way.

We were having a great time, but we knew in our heart of hearts that this was just temporary. A year and a half had passed, and we were driving to Texas to explore a business opportunity when Bob saw a billboard off the highway that caught his eye. He looked it up and discovered that it was a business that helped people build their own homes. He found in the last year that he loved homes and construction, but his true calling was sales and marketing. Bob could help people find land using my contacts in real estate, he could help them with financing, assist them in figuring out their plans with the help of an architect, and with the leadership of some incredible construction consultants, he could play a part in other people achieving their own dreams. We bought a franchise with the little money we had left, and began a new business and a new dream. God is so good. He gave us the opportunity, the time to learn so we could be prepared, the means to purchase the franchise, and the ability to serve our community. Our Oklahoma City franchise is His. It was all in His plan for us, but we had to wait. He had things He needed to teach us about real estate, about construction, but mostly about faith.

"Wait patiently for the Lord. Be brave and courageous. Yes, wait patiently on the Lord" (Psalm 27:14, NLT). I have a friend who shared with me what this verse means to her. She said that often we think of patiently waiting on God as passive or cowardly, but this verse paints a very different picture. *Because* this verse calls for us to be brave and courageous, she envisions an army of mighty soldiers with their swords and shields raised, ready and anticipating action, and then victory. I wonder if we viewed waiting patiently as a diligent and proactive act of valor, it might transform our own perspective on the importance and virtue of godly patience.

Today our business has grown tremendously. We have opened two more franchises and in 2011, Bob and a fellow franchisee partnered to buy the national office. Did I say God is good? God's dreams for us are so much bigger than we can even conceive.

But what would have happened if we hadn't waited on God? Sure, God would still have provided for us, but because we went off half-cocked with our *own* plans it wouldn't have been *His* best for us. Now I don't want to mislead you, I described patience a few pages ago as "the ability to wait with grace." I wasn't always graceful. I waited and tried diligently to rest in the hands of Jesus, but my human side would occasionally win a battle or two or a hundred. But really, who's counting? I would sometimes become very anxious about the future, my four children, my security; and complain that we needed to figure things out *now*! Looking back, I'm regretful of those moments, but I know they were simply growing pains.

Since then, waiting is easier and easier. I can wait on God. Why? Practice. Patience is a learned trait. It's the rare individual that is just naturally patient. God is teaching it to me even today.

> Can you describe a situation in your own life when God was asking you to be still and wait?
>
> _____
>
> _____
>
> _____
>
> In what ways did deciding to wait on God transform you?
>
> _____
>
> _____

COURAGE TO PERSEVERE

Now, what about endurance? When I asked my class to define endurance, the answers were precise. "Don't give up." "Have hope." "Don't trust in your circumstances… trust in God." The word *endurance* gives me chills because I know what it means. It means that something really awful is going to happen, and I am going to have to learn to persevere through the pain. I'm sorry, but I'm a big 'fraidy cat by nature. I don't *want* to have to endure. I, like all people, want life to be happy and light and fun. Although, I do have to admit that it *is* the hard times that make me better. Rats!

Here is what the Bible has to say about endurance:

> We can rejoice, too, when we run into problems
> and trials, for we know that they are good

for us—they help us to learn to endure. And endurance develops strength of character in us, and character strengthens our confident expectation of salvation. And this expectation will not disappoint us. For we know how dearly God loves us, because He has given us the Holy Spirit to fill our hearts with His love.

Romans 5:3–5 (NLT)

Dear brothers and sisters, whenever trouble comes your way, let it be an opportunity for joy. For when your faith is tested, your endurance has a chance to grow. So let it grow, for when your endurance is fully developed, you will be strong in character and ready for anything.

James 1:2–4 (NLT)

Did you guys catch that? Not only am I supposed to be faithful that God really will take care of me when trouble comes; I'm supposed to be happy about it. That takes endurance in itself. Making the decision to accept hardship as a blessing and an honor...well, just writing that makes me exhausted. That alone *is* endurance. Solomon wrote in Ecclesiastes a verse that jolts me a little bit every time I read it: "Sorrow is better than laughter, for sadness has a refining influence on us" (Ecclesiastes 7:3, NLT). Sorrow is better than laughter? Huh? Now surely Solomon didn't like weeping more than laughing, but sorrow made him more faithful, wiser, stronger...better. He knew that. It doesn't mean he necessarily enjoyed it, but he didn't hasten it away because he knew that whatever sorrow was allowed in his life would be used for his refinement. So he chose to endure. What happens if we endure? We grow. Our character is strengthened, and our faith is renewed—just like Solomon, his father David, Noah, Abraham, Joseph, Moses, Jacob, Daniel, Isaiah, Jeremiah, Hosea, Ruth, Esther, and countless others. *Greatness was the result* of their endurance. My pastor has said, "The road to spiritual maturity isn't paved with rainbows and unicorns…the road to spiritual maturity is paved with struggle."

What is your first response to terrible situations?

_____

_____

Can you describe positive character traits that God developed in you through difficult circumstances?

_____

_____

TO SPIRAL OR STAND

You know the old saying, "Whatever doesn't kill you makes you stronger"? Well, that statement isn't entirely true. When hardships come, we have a choice. We can look to God and say, "Okay. I don't know what you're doing or why you're doing it, but I will follow you no matter what comes my way. Show me the path through the darkness." Or we can do what a large majority do—spiral. We reject God in our distress, we run to the world instead of Him. The world will not make you stronger. The world makes you weaker, if it doesn't kill you. Your enemy knows this. Don't be fooled when tragedy strikes.

You will be tempted to blame God, to isolate yourself from those who want to minister to you, to rebel. Choose God instead. Romans 8:28 (NLT) says, "And we know that God causes all things to work together for good of those who love Him and are called according to His purpose for them." He really will take your heartache and make a masterpiece of it if you let Him.

I have a friend named Diana. She has been battling cancer for seven years. She has endured multiple experimental treatments, chemotherapy, and countless operations. I lost count of how many times she's lost her hair. As often as she is able, we get together for lunch, and she blows me away with some of the statements she makes. Endurance has made her wise and strong. I want to share with you a few.

When she was a girl, she accepted Christ as her savior. As an adult, she married her sweet husband, Joe. Joe could make friends with a tree stump. They had a son named Matt who at the time was eight. Our sons played little league football together. As we got to know them, we found they were un-churched. Around the same time, Diana was diagnosed with cancer. Diana wanted to be back in church, so they visited ours. Our church family embraced them. It is so beautiful to watch the body of Christ at work. Through this, Joe and Matt came to know the Lord in a very meaningful way and were baptized together. Wow! Diana thanks God for her cancer. She knows her cancer will enable her to be with her husband and son forever. Can you imagine thanking God for a life threatening illness? She does. All the time. Continually.

100

There was a time when she went into remission. During that short interval, people said to her, including myself, "You finally get to have your life back." She replied simply, "I always had a great life. It was just a different kind of life." She still had joy in the midst of painful treatments, operations, and uncertainty. That's God at work.

Last one. The last time we had lunch, she said, "You know, I guess I could ask God, 'Why me?' But 'why *not* me?'" I'm astounded by that kind of grace. I'm in awe of that kind of character. Diana will tell you she has had plenty of pity parties, but she lives to fight, love, and rejoice another day.

In Psalm 31, David wrote some very poetic words about his own suffering,

> I am overcome with joy because of your unfailing love, for you have seen my troubles, and you care about the anguish of my soul. You have not handed me over to my enemy, but have set me in a safe place. Have mercy on me, Lord, for I am in distress. My sight is blurred because of my tears. My body and soul are withering away. I am dying from grief; my years are shortened by sadness. Misery has drained my strength; I am wasting away from within. I am scorned by all my enemies and despised by my neighbors-even my friends are afraid to come near me. When they see me on the street, they turn the other way. I have been ignored as if I were dead, as if I were a broken pot. I have heard many rumors about me, and I am surrounded by terror. My enemies conspire

against me, plotting to take my life. But I am trusting you, oh Lord, saying 'You are my God.'"

Psalm 31:7–14 (NLT)

Now David was experiencing some serious anguish, but did you catch what he said at the end? This is crucial. He said, *"But I am trusting you, oh Lord, saying you are my God."*

Are you saying in the face a great hardship or tragedy, "But I am trusting you, oh Lord, saying you are my God"? Give it a try. Right now. Just say that to Him. Just saying those words brings an oasis of peace. You might have to say it again in an hour, but keep saying it. Say it as much as you have need. "I am trusting you, I am trusting you, I am trusting you." Patient endurance will blossom, and with it, will come beauty and peace and wisdom and joy. Can you believe that? Joy will come through pain. "Weeping may go on all night, but joy comes with the morning" (Psalm 30:5, NLT).

Have you ever chosen to spiral into darkness when trouble came?

_____

What was the result?

_____

_____

Are you going through the valley right now? Are you choosing to trust God? In what ways are you growing?

_____

_____

_____

"…let us lay aside every weight and sin that so easily ensnare us. Let us run with endurance the race that lies before us."

Hebrews 12:1b (NLT)

WEEK SEVEN

GODLINESS
STEP 6: "PATIENT ENDURANCE LEADS TO GODLINESS"

"So make every effort to apply the benefits of
these promises to your life. Then your faith will
produce a life of moral excellence. A life of moral
excellence leads to knowing God better. Knowing
God better leads to self-control. Self-control
leads to patient endurance, and patient endurance
leads to godliness."

2 Peter 1:5–6

ssiduous...great word. The dictionary definition
of *assiduous* is "constant; unremitting; constant in
application or effort; persevering; industrious; attentive."
Constant in love, constant in faith, constant in seeking,
constant in study, constant in the face of persecution—
these are the character traits that lead to godliness. Like I

said, great word. God teaches us to be assiduous through opportunity, through trials, through His Word, through our own uncertainty. This past year, I have experienced some uncertainty. We all do. None of us know the future or what it holds. We can find ourselves unable to sleep at night, worrying about how to handle tomorrow. We spend so much time asking God for signs and audible commands so we will know in which direction to move. "God, why can't you just talk to me like you did to Moses? No burning bushes, no thunderous voice from the heaven giving me detailed instruction. What's up?"

He actually does give us detailed instruction. There is a verse that I have held very dear to my heart this year as I have been trying to make some pretty big life decisions. "I pondered the direction of my life, and I turned to follow your statutes. I will hurry, without lingering, to obey your commands" (Psalm 119:59–60, NLT). Obey His commands. It really is that simple. Are you tempted to cheat on your taxes? Don't. Do you really want to "shoot the bird" to that guy who cut you off on the highway? Keep both hands on the steering wheel. Do you really want to tell your cousin that you have the flu so you don't have to go to a "See my vacation to Spain slide show" party? Just tell them you're perfectly well, but no one wants to see their pictures. Say this in love, of course. Trust me; your other relatives will thank you later. My point is, stay away from sin and God will reveal His plan. He will drop the bread crumbs and you will follow.

Now, please don't misunderstand. God is not bargaining with you. He is not saying, "If you scratch my back, I'll scratch yours." Your incentive for doing godly things should not be motivated by your selfish need for the answers to your future. God is simply saying that when your life is holy, then you're focused on me. When your focused on me, then you can hear me, you can see my hand in your life. Your eyes are open to my activity. When your life is habitually sinful, you can't hear Him, you can't see Him.

I discovered this prayer written in a Bible study. I make it a point to say it regularly. "Lord, today let me see you when you are moving and hear you when you are speaking. Heighten my spiritual sensitivities to notice your activity around me, to me, and through me to others. May your presence become so evident this day that I am steered clear of mistakes that I would most assuredly make left to my own natural tendencies. Give me, dear Lord, a consciousness, and awareness of you everywhere and anywhere I go."

In this prayer, you are asking God to take control. You ask God to heighten your spiritual sensitivities so that with his presence so close, you would be steered away from sins that you would normally commit without even blinking an eye. I am not motivated to please God because I want to know all the answers, but when confronted with temptation, I do remember that verse from Psalms. I need His help. I need His answers, His timing, His wisdom. My need for God to guide my life steers me away from sin.

What would happen to your fear and worry if you applied Psalms 119:59–60 to every confusing dilemma in your life?

_____

_____

In what ways do you desire to see God's movement in your life right now?

_____

_____

IGNORANCE IS BLISS

Steering yourself away from sin demonstrates serious perseverance. But keeping ourselves ignorant of sin is the best way to endure. One day, I was reading in Genesis about the fall of man into sin. I'd heard this story my whole life and read it many times before, but that day I was surprised by something new that God was revealing to me. Genesis chapter 3 begins like this:

> "Really," he asked the woman. "Did God really say you must not eat any of the fruit in the garden?" "Of course we may eat." The woman told him. "It's only the fruit from the tree at the center of the garden that we are not allowed to eat. God says we must not eat it or even touch it, or we will die." "You won't die!" the serpent hissed. "God knows that your eyes will be opened when you eat it. You will become just like God, knowing everything, both good and evil." The woman was convinced. The fruit looked so fresh and delicious, and it would make her so wise! So she ate some of the

fruit. She also gave some to her husband, who was with her. Then he ate it, too. At that moment, their eyes were opened, and they suddenly felt shame at their nakedness. So they strung fig leaves together around their hips to cover themselves.

Genesis 3:1–7 (NLT)

What was Eve's state of mind right before she was convinced to eat the fruit? Well, she seemed to have been feeling a bit betrayed that God had been trying to pull the wool over her eyes. She was definitely feeling rebellious; otherwise, she wouldn't have eaten the fruit. And what about Adam? He was standing right beside Eve, and without a word or thought, he took the fruit and ate. Wasn't it his job to lead? So did Adam and Eve sin even before they ate the fruit? I was having one of those brain meltdowns. "How can this be? If sin entered the world when they ate the apple, or *because* they ate the apple, then how can we explain their sin-like emotions and thoughts before they actually took a bite?" Well, the answer surfaced very quickly. First, I remembered the name of the tree. It was called the tree of the *knowledge* of good and evil, and the name of the tree has all the relevance in the world. Then I thought of Paul's words to the Romans in chapter 7 beginning in verse 5:

> When we were controlled by our old nature, sinful desires were at work within us, and the law aroused these evil desires that produced sinful deeds, resulting in death. But now we have been released from the law, for we died with Christ, and we are no longer captive to its power. Now we can really serve God, not in the old way by

obeying the letter of the law, but in the new way, by the Spirit. Well then, am I suggesting that the law of God is evil? Of course not! The law is not sinful, but it was the law that showed me my sin. I would never have known that coveting is wrong if the law had not said, 'Do not covet.' But sin took advantage of the law and aroused all kinds of forbidden desires within me! If there were no law, sin would not have that power.

Romans 7:5–8 (NLT)

These scriptures help us to understand that while God's law is perfect and good, that even *knowing* it "arouses all kinds of forbidden desires." My grandpa told me a hilarious story illustrating this point beautifully. He was the oldest of five very rowdy siblings. When he was growing up, he had a large mulberry tree in his front yard. He and his siblings were going out to play one summer day, and as they were leaving the house, their mother yelled out to them (obviously kidding), "Don't stick those mulberries up your nose." *Lightbulb!* Can you guess what happened next? Three of the five siblings were at the doctor's office later that afternoon with nostrils full of mulberries. Now, you can bet your bottom dollar that if my great grandmother had not shouted those infamous last words, the thought of shoving mulberries up their noses would have never even crossed their minds. But just the knowledge, just the awareness, just the curiosity— well, that dastardly temptation could not be dissuaded.

This is in no way some sort of excuse to not know God's law. God's law reveals our sin to us. We need the law, but Paul was trying to help us understand just how weak our flesh can be and why keeping our hearts and minds pure is crucial to avoiding sin.

The knowledge of sin breeds temptation that is impossible to combat without the strength of an almighty God. Sin entered the world through the knowledge that had been gained from partaking of the fruit. Adam and Eve weren't mindless robots programmed to obey God. They *chose* to obey Him. They had personalities and emotions and passions. If they didn't, then that serpent could never have persuaded them. They weren't perfect, they were still human, but they were humans without any knowledge of sin. And with one bite, their eyes were opened. They knew sin and therefore would never be able to be free from the bondage of that knowledge.

This answered so many questions that I had struggled with during my Christian walk. Have you ever thought, "Why is this or that sin such an ongoing, tireless temptation for me?" When I was a teenager, I was a habitual liar. I lied just for my own entertainment. I lied when there was no threat of retribution. I just lied all the time. When I decided to follow Jesus with my whole heart, I began to feel a strong conviction to tell the truth. As time has passed, I am happy to say I am not a habitual liar. I tell the truth. Sometimes I'm accused of telling too much truth. Nevertheless, while I don't have an ongoing temptation to lie, I do have an ever-present, knowing awareness of that sin. Why? Because I have so much knowledge of that sin.

I also still struggle with my language. Twenty years ago, as I wrote earlier, I had a filthy mouth. Today, I'm happy to say I am not habitually profane. But when you jostle this cup, sometimes nasty things spew out. When I stump my toe, you won't hear words like "Shucks! Ouch! Rats!" I'm not proud of this, but I am honest, per the above paragraph. Why am I still tempted to use foul language? Because I have knowledge of it.

Or what about what we let the world reveal to us by what we watch, hear, and read? There is an old saying that "Art imitates life." While there are examples to support that theory, I, for the most part, disagree. I think in so many ways, life imitates art. When you were a teenager, did you ever just try to mimic the image you saw of other teenagers represented in movies? Honestly, those movies are what opened the door to my "partying" years. Have you ever watched TV shows and thought, *I will never be able to un-see that?* Your mind was opened to something perverse and wicked. It might have been entertaining, but in some way, it stole some purity from you. When I was a young woman, the mother of a dear friend of mine read a very popular novel about a married woman with three children who found "true love" with another man in her forties. Within a month, my friend's Christian mother left her husband of over twenty years, citing that she never really loved him. I'm not saying that this book was their only problem, but it definitely opened the door to entertain sin.

Keeping myself and my family pure of heart took on a whole new meaning. The more ignorant I am of sin, the less temptation I will face. If I'm tempted less, it only stands to reason, that I will sin less. In this instance, be as ignorant as you can. Be as pure as a child. "Blessed are those who are pure of heart, for they shall see God" (Matthew 5:8, NLT).

> "I will refuse to look at anything vile and vulgar." Psalm 101:3a (NLT)
>
> In what ways are you keeping yourself ignorant of sin?
>
> _____
> _____
>
> What are two things that your eyes see and your ears hear that are giving you knowledge of sin?
>
> _____
> _____
>
> Would you be willing to give them up?
>
> _____
> _____

IS IT TOO LATE FOR ME?

The endurance that is required in this wicked world to remain pure, to remain ignorant of sin, will absolutely breed godliness. To stand, to fight the good fight, to walk through the valley of the shadow of death and remain unstained.

Now, what about those of us who are more "stained" than most? There are some of us who have lived like the heroines of the Bible—Ruth, Elizabeth, Esther—and then there are those of us who were more like Mary Magdalene, Jezebel, Delilah. Is there hope for the "bad girls"? Are you feeling disheartened? Are you thinking, "Wow, I have so much knowledge of sin, how will I ever feel like I can be pure and free from the temptations that have crippled me in the past?" Well, Jezebel and Delilah never experienced freedom, but Mary Magdalene sure did. She accepted the love and forgiveness Jesus came to give her. She *really* believed that when He said she was as white as snow, that she was as white as snow. From scripture, we know that Mary never returned to her old life. She became a devout follower of the one who freed her. Her endurance was probably the most inspiring. She had knowledge of *a lot* of sin, and yet she made every effort to apply the benefits of her salvation. Her faith produced a life of moral excellence, which led to knowing God better. Then knowing God led to self-control, and her self-control led to patient endurance, and that endurance led to godliness.

Your sin that paralyzed you can now be your greatest triumph. Overcoming the knowledge of sin in your life can be your most influential testimony. The Apostle Paul would definitely tell you that truth. He was bitter and angry and full of venom. He beat Christians, imprisoned them, and even authorized their murders. And yet, with all his knowledge of violence and hate, he was completely transformed by Jesus's grace. When I consider all the sin from which God has delivered me, I'm overwhelmed. Micah 7:19 (NLT) says, "Once again you have compassion on us. You will trample our sins under your feet and throw them into the depths of the ocean." I don't even remotely resemble the girl I used to be. God has transformed me. I have knowledge of sin, but the more I seek God, the more He seems to erase my memory of that darkness. My heart is pure, and I am as white as snow.

You might have knowledge of great sin, but God has greater forgiveness. Is there knowledge of sin that still haunts you? What is it?

_____

_____

It's going to take some serious mind transformation to feel free, because your enemy wants you to feel ashamed and helpless. What can you do today, to begin to break the chains of your knowledge of sin?

_____

_____

_____

WEEK EIGHT

GOD'S LOVE

STEPS 7 AND 8: "GODLINESS LEADS TO LOVE FOR OTHER CHRISTIANS. AND FINALLY YOU WILL GROW TO HAVE A GENUINE LOVE FOR EVERYONE."

So make every effort to apply the benefits of these promises to your life. Then your faith will produce a life of moral excellence. A life of moral excellence leads to knowing God better. Knowing God better leads to self-control. Self-control leads to patient endurance and patient endurance leads to godliness. Godliness leads to love for other Christians, and finally you will grow to have genuine love for everyone.

2 Peter 1:5–8 (NLT)

Hmm…love. Love seems so easy, doesn't it? It's natural to love. We love our spouses. We love our children. We love our parents. We love our friends. We love our pets. We love genuinely and fully. Done. Chapter complete. Well, wait. Let's first examine the definition of love as described in scripture.

First Corinthians 13:4–7 (NLT) says…

> Love is patient and kind. Love is not jealous or boastful or proud or rude. Love does not demand its own way. Love is not irritable, and it keeps no record of when it has been wronged. It is never glad about injustice but rejoices whenever truth wins out. Love never gives up, never loses faith, is always hopeful, and endures through every circumstance.

Now let's try a little exercise. Replace your name in the place of love.

Sarena is patient and kind. Sarena is not jealous or boastful or proud or rude. Sarena does not demand her own way. Sarena is not irritable, and she keeps no record of when she has been wronged. Sarena is never glad about injustice, but rejoices whenever truth wins out. Sarena never gives up, she never loses faith, she is always hopeful, and she endures through every circumstance.

Yikes! I can't tell you how many times I cringed as I was writing that paragraph. Evidently, "love" is not as easy as the *world* would have you think. No wonder Peter had to *teach* people that it would take a journey of surrendering to the Holy Spirit before we would really be able to love people the way God intended us to.

As I mentioned above, it is really natural to love people who love us. In Matthew 5:47–48 (NLT), Jesus tells us that even "corrupt tax collectors do that much. If you are kind to only your friends, how are you different from anyone else? Even pagans do that. But you are to be perfect, even as your Father in heaven is perfect."

So we love our kids, we love our spouse, we love our friends, we love our pets—so what? How hard is that? That's child's play! Which leads me to this conclusion: God's love is different than human love. I mean, that's not a big surprise, but I don't think we, as believers, spend much time pondering what God's love *is*, and how we can mimic it.

How many of us would tolerate hate, indifference, adultery, betrayal, insults, and rejection, and then still be waiting with open arms for our offender? Now take it a step further; allow your child to be killed for the sake of that offender. That is God's love. Unfathomable.

So unfathomable that I will be honest with you; I'm not there yet. I'm on my journey, I'm growing, I'm surrendering, but I'm not there yet. I have glimpses of that kind of love. There are moments when I experience God's love pouring out of me, but it's not me. They are instances when I am so surrendered to the Holy Spirit that He just uses me like a vessel, and I almost feel like I'm having an out-of-body experience. In those minutes, I feel a supernatural joy that cannot be expressed in words. There has even been a three to four-year season in my life when God was so loud, that hearing Him was virtually effortless, being faithful was virtually effortless, and love was virtually effortless. But lately, I've been in a spiritual drought. God is not silent, but He has been quiet. Man, that is a serious faith tester. Feelings of loneliness and desertion rear their ugly head, and it feels like everything is a struggle. Reading God's Word, trusting Him, believing that He cares, loving people who don't necessarily love me—it's all a challenge. You know a verse that gets me through that time? I shared it earlier. Psalm 31:7 (NLT) says, "I am overcome with joy because of your unfailing love, for you have seen my troubles, and you care about the anguish of my soul." Just being reminded that God is with me, He knows me, and He cares about me, gives me the strength to keep on keeping on. I keep on seeking, and I keep on loving, even though it's not coming naturally. God really is using this time in my life, in your life, to prepare you for His greater plan. Hold on.

If you ponder the ways that God loves us, how is it different from the way you love?

_____

_____

In response to the above question, a friend of mine answered it, hitting the nail on the head. God doesn't have to *try* to love or *think* about ways to love…He just loves, because He *is* love.

How do you cope when faithfulness and love are not effortless?

_____

_____

SO. WHAT'S THE DIFFERENCE?

Peter separates love into two steps. He first says that the godliness developed in us will lead us to love other Christians, and *then* we will grow to love all people. So what's the difference between loving a believer and loving a non-believer?

Well, what are the differences between believers and non-believers? We are both humans, we both have emotions, we both can think, we are both capable of love and goodness, we both are capable of wickedness. We both work for a living—buy homes, raise families, pay taxes, retire, and die. So how are we so different?

Believers know that they have been saved by grace. They know that there is hope for the future. They have assurance that they will live forever in heaven. They hopefully know the purpose for their life, and it is to walk with God, discovering His mission for their lives, and then pursuing it. Most importantly, the Holy Spirit lives in each believer. This great counselor changes our perspectives, our behavior, our values, and our relationships. The Holy Spirit unites people into a family of single-mindedness.

> Therefore I (Paul), a prisoner for serving the Lord, beg you to lead a life worthy of your calling, for you have been called by God. Be humble and gentle. Be patient with each other, making allowance for each other's faults because of your love. Always keep yourselves united in the Holy Spirit, and bind yourselves together with peace. We are all one body, we have the same Spirit,

> and we have all been called to the same glorious future. There is only one Lord, one faith, one baptism, and there is only one God and Father, who is over us all and in us all and living through us all. He has given each one of us a special gift according to the generosity of Christ.
>
> Ephesians 4:1–7 (NLT)

Based on this, it's evident why it is easier to love other Christians rather than non-Christians. Have you ever been a long way from home, in a place very different from home, with people who are very different from you? Then suddenly, across the street, or sitting in the booth next to yours, or standing in the check-out line, you see someone wearing a University of Oklahoma (replace with your home state) sweat shirt. Someone from home! Someone who gets you! Someone who feels like home! You rush to that person, your eyes meet, as you quickly blurt out, "Are you from Oklahoma?" They excitedly smile and reply, "Yes! Are you?" For the next ten minutes, you engage in conversation about what neighborhood you live in, where your kids go to school, where you work, and how you bet your second cousin knows their bosses' aunt. It's familiar. You walk away feeling encouraged, knowing that there is someone out there who "gets" you. You're connected.

It's the same for believers. We seek each other out. We have so much in common even if we have nothing in common. We belong to a united family, and we are connected. And yet, we fail. We judge, criticize, and even loathe other believers. How does this happen? We were having such a love fest with our unity in Christ and all!

In a few lines, explain the differences in a relationship that you have with a believer and a non-believer.

_____

_____

In what ways do you feel united to other Christians, and in what ways do you feel Christians separate themselves from one another?

_____

_____

_____

I'M OFFENDED!

Hmm…well, it just takes someone rubbing you the wrong way with a thoughtless word, or disagreeing with your perfectly correct theology, or someone irritating you with their bossiness to be utterly offended. Or it can get even worse—churches split, friendships are destroyed, and wounds that are so debilitating it takes years to recover from; all occur at the hands of Christians. See, God's love is not so easy for us mere humans. You know why? Because we are so easily offended. We love ourselves so much that we cannot fathom the idea that someone could—criticize me, ignore me, disagree with me, or order me around. God's love is *not* easily offended.

We live in a hypersensitive world, especially with the onset of the "politically correct" movement that began evolving into the monster it has become since the late 1980s. People are not allowed to be themselves, we are not allowed to share what is in our hearts, men are not allowed to be men; women are not allowed to be women lest we offend someone. That choke hold is killing love. We are being so strangled by the philosophies of our world that would tell you "political correctness" *is* love. "It's fostering tolerance and kindness." No! No! No! It is actually having the absolute opposite effect. It's killing tolerance and it's definitely stifling love. Because it is only acceptable to express thoughts that are within the perimeters of our so-called tolerant society *and* our churches; so when we experience a moment of real truth and we want to express it, we are shut down because "political correctness" has no "tolerance" for such epiphanies. Even if our thoughts are raw and dark, but they're real, we are just too afraid to be honest because people will be offended. And being offended quenches God's love. It in turn makes us weaker. Because we are offended by so much, so often, it makes it difficult to let things just roll off of our back, which results in resentment, bitterness, and ineffectiveness. We waste so much time stewing about what people *shouldn't have said* that we squander God's precious productivity time. So Betty Sue said she didn't care for your flower arrangement. *So what?* So that new kid in the youth group curses a lot. *Who cares?* God will convict him. He doesn't need you to do His job, and he certainly doesn't need you to be shocked and dismayed. I know this sounds strange, but we need to toughen up so we can learn to love like Jesus. How do we reach a lost world if we are always so horribly aghast and offended by it? How will we love each other, let alone the world, if we're so lost in a fog of hypersensitivity?

I knew this boy at church who was a believer. He loved the Lord, but he had lapses in good judgment (same as you and me). He text this slightly off color joke to a group of kids in our youth group. I'm not going to lie. It was tacky. But the uproar of offended kids and parents was ridiculous. They judged him and ignored him because of it. They refused to love him because they were offended. What? How can we love sinners, if we can't even love our own?

Jesus was tough. He hung with the prostitutes, the thieves, the liars, and even the hypocritical Pharisees. I'm sure the language at the tax collectors table wasn't always so prim and proper. I'm almost certain that the beggars and prostitutes made inappropriate remarks. Did that stop Jesus from loving them? No! He could love them because He wasn't offended by them.

I'm not trying to imply that there are no conditions that should be offensive to us. There are. But let's not get all wrapped up in the "small stuff"—that is a battle currently being won by our enemy. Decide to not be offended. When someone says something nasty or even just slightly disagreeable, and you begin to feel that ire rise up in your throat, smile. Don't tell anyone. That only amplifies the problem. Don't spend any time thinking about it. That only breeds contempt. Don't judge them and believe that they are not suited for Christian service. Be like Ebenezer Scrooge's nephew, Fred, from *A Christmas Carol*. You just couldn't offend that guy! Ebenezer Scrooge was horrible to him, but he always blew it off with a smile. He could love Scrooge because he did not allow himself to be offended by Scrooge.

Okay. Let's test ourselves.

What kinds of things offend you? (Negativity, arrogance, bluntness...)

_____

_____

Can you describe the last time someone offended you?

_____

_____

Did you stew about it? Did you tell someone else about the incident? Did that decrease or increase your resentment?

_____

_____

What would have happened if we reacted like Scrooge's nephew? Would you be a happier person? Would the offender be a happier person? Would the people in your sphere of influence benefit from your response?

_____

_____

THEY MIGHT GIVE ME COOTIES!

Our human tendency to be so easily offended definitely translates into love—or rather, lack of love—for the unbeliever. You know Scripture tells us in First Corinthians chapter 5 how absurd it is for us to judge unbelievers.

> When I (Paul) wrote you before, I told you not to associate with people who indulge in sexual sin. But I wasn't talking about *unbelievers* who indulge

in sexual sin, or who are greedy, or are swindlers, or idol worshipers. You would have to leave this world to avoid people like that. What I meant was that you are not to associate with anyone who claims to be a Christian yet indulges in sexual sin, or is greedy, or worships idols, or is abusive, or a drunkard, or a swindler. Don't even eat with such people. It isn't my (Paul) responsibility to judge outsiders, but it certainly is your job to judge those inside the church who are sinning in these ways.

1 Corinthians 5:9–12 (NLT)

Now before any confusion erupts, Paul is talking about sin that should offend us. Earlier in this same chapter, Paul instructs the church to deal swiftly with a member of this congregation who was openly involved in a sexual relationship with his stepmother. Galatians 6:1 says that we are to go to a Christian brother or sister who is "overcome" by sin and help them back on to the right path. Incestuous adultery definitely falls into that category. My point is that we shouldn't be picking other Christians apart over menial flaws. Ephesians 4:2 (NLT) says, "Be humble and gentle. Be patient with each other, making allowance for each other's faults because of your love."

Now, back to my earlier point: we shouldn't be judging non-believers *at all.* They don't know what they don't know. Paul was correcting the Corinthian church for judging outsiders by Christian morality. You can't condemn someone for a standard they haven't yet acquired. And we wonder why the world mocks Christians, calling us judgmental hate mongers. Hmm. If the shoe fits...

I do understand Peter's point. We are more capable of loving Christians because we do, for the most part, have the same standards. In commanding us to love the world, we absolutely must learn to separate the sin that is supposed to offend us from the actual wonderfully made workmanship of God, His lost creation. The lost are not diseased, they are just lost. They need us to see past the offensive sin. They need us to not be offended and love them.

The band Casting Crowns sings this amazing song called "Jesus, Friend of Sinners," and the lyrics convict me to the core:

> Jesus, friend of sinners, we have strayed so far away. We cut down people in your name, but the sword was never ours to swing. Jesus, friend of sinners, the truth's become so hard to see, the world is on their way to You, but they're tripping over me. Always looking around but never looking up I'm so double minded, a plank eyed saint with dirty hands and a heart divided
>
> Oh Jesus, friend of sinners, open our eyes to the world at the end of our pointing fingers. Let our hearts be led by mercy, help us reach with open hearts and open doors. Oh Jesus, friend of sinners, break our hearts for what breaks yours.
>
> Jesus, friend of sinners, the one who's writing in the sand, made the righteous turn away and the stones fall from their hands. Help us to remember we are all the least of these. Let the memory of Your mercy bring Your people to their

knees. Nobody knows what we're for, only what
we're against when we judge the wounded. What
if we put down our signs, crossed over the lines,
and loved like You did.

You love every lost cause; you reach for the
outcast, for the leper and the lame; they're the
reason that You came. Lord I was that lost cause
and I was the outcast, but you died for sinners just
like me, a grateful leper at Your feet

Cause You are good, You are good and Your
love endures forever.

There is hope. If Jesus loved you, bled for you, died
for you, rose again for you, forgave you, saved you, and
lives in you, surely you can love the least of these. I'm
not saying it's easy. It's not. Here is what *is* easy—loving
God. Let Him do the rest. He is so ready to grow you
into what He already knows you are. Take the leap. Let
Him. Let us all remember that at some point of our lives,
we were the outcast. We have been saved by merciful,
unfathomable grace, that we would not forget the hurting
and the lonely. That we would use the love God planted
in us to find the lost, and heal the wounded in His name.

So make every effort to apply the benefits of His
promises to your life. Then that faith will produce moral
excellence. That moral excellence will lead you to knowing
God. Knowing God will lead to self-control. Self-control
will lead to patient endurance. Patient endurance will
lead to godliness. And godliness will lead to love, great
love, love that changes your life and the lives of all who
know you. "As we know Jesus better, His divine power
gives us everything we need for living a godly life. He has

called us to receive His own glory and goodness" (2 Peter 1:3, NLT).

"The steps of the godly are directed by the Lord, He delights in every detail of their lives. Though they stumble, they will not fall, for the Lord holds them by the hand" (Psalm 37:23–24, NLT).

LEADER GUIDE

I am so happy that you have decided to be a leader to women in your sphere of influence. My hope is that this short guide will give you some applicable techniques to equip you for leading this study. Each week you will be reviewing the material and the study questions. You're goal as a leader is to help enable women to feel comfortable, safe, and open, so that God's heart for them is revealed in a mighty way.

- Pray over the study, pray over the women as a group and individually, and pray that God would supply you with His leadership, as you look forward to new growth and Christian friendship.
- Reserve a meeting place and arrange for childcare if it is needed.
- Begin promoting the study in your church and community. Get the word out.
- Have books available for each member at the first meeting.

- You might want to ask someone to provide refreshments. Iced tea and chocolate chip cookies always lend to a relaxed and warm environment.
- If you anticipate that you will have a group larger than 15, you might want to split into smaller groups of 6-8, and enlist small group leaders to help facilitate. Ask God to direct you to the women He would have lead. Leaders need to understand that they will not be "teaching", but encouraging spiritually healthy and judgment free conversation.

YOUR FIRST MEETING

- Come prepared. Be familiar with the material.
- Distribute books to the members.
- Hand out a Bible Study Schedule with all the dates and times you will be meeting.
- Pass around a sign-up sheet. Have women provide their email addresses and phone numbers.
- Pass out a Prayer request sheet. This way each woman can list her prayer needs and then they can be sent out to the group via email each week.
- Introduce yourself, share your testimony, and explain what has led you to lead this study.
- Give the women confident assurance that this is a safe environment to share their hearts.
- Ask each woman to introduce herself and give a few adjectives that would best describe her personality, or have the women split into groups of two and ask them to interview each other.

Supply questions that they might ask, and then have them each introduce their interview partner to the group. These are always fun icebreakers. Your goal is to help them become acquainted and comfortable. When women feel accepted and loved, they will keep coming back.

- Describe what you will be doing each week. The participants will read each week's chapter and answer the study questions. Encourage them to really ponder the questions and take time to answer authentically. When you meet you will give an overview of each section and you will ask some, if not all, of the study questions. Then you will guide the discussion and try to always monitor the clock so you can end on time.
- Close in prayer.

YOUR SECOND AND ALL SUBSEQUENT MEETINGS

- Ask God to lead each week directing you to ask the study questions that are most important to this individual group.
- Begin in prayer and ask God to open your hearts, your ears, and your spiritual eyes that you might hear God speaking.
- Let the Holy Spirit do His work. God will move, so make sure you always have tissue available.
- Try to stick to the material. Sometimes the conversations will drift into other subjects, but as a leader you will need to be able to steer the conversation back to topic.

- Love on these ladies relentlessly. Encourage them to send notes, emails, and text messages to one another. This will help create a group who reaches out and lifts one another up. Through this, God will develop a dynamic group of women who love and bear each other's burdens. Be careful. This group will be a light that shines in the darkness, so expect and welcome growth.

God bless you, and I'm praying that your group is one that is transformed by the unfathomable love of Jesus.